– July, 1988 –

Happy Birthday Ryan; I hope
it's as special as you are!
Thanks for sharing your beautiful
city with me – I look forward
to sharing you mine.

Best wishes,
Jan Hamilton

Derik Murray

Tom Sutherland

This book was made possible by:

 Canadian Tire

Kodak Canada Inc.

THE WESTIN BAYSHORE
Vancouver

Vancouver City Savings
Credit Union

Lens & Shutter

GARIBALDI
GRAPHICS

abc photocolour

 Official book of the
Vancouver Centennial

Vancouver had a less than encouraging beginning. Six weeks after its incorporation as a city one hundred years ago, the tiny clot of buildings that was to becom this thriving hub was reduced to a pile of smoking rub ble. If every great city must have its fire, then the blaze of 1886 at least brought one consolation—it put Vancouver on the map.

Although that fire took us off the map momentarily, we have gone on to become a city of distinction I like to think of Vancouver as a success story. We have spawned innumerable international sporting figures, noted entertainers, doggedly successful business types the odd politician, and quite a few fish. We are a group of eccentrics—you may have guessed that. We've had a salaried fool, a peanut that was nearly the mayor, and we continue to hold in esteem the host of people who thunder headlong into the Pacific Ocean on January 1st each year to take a refreshing, if brief, swim.

With the ambitious Expo 86 as our centrepiece and the subject of our great attention, 1985 was truly a year like no other. The energy in the air was palpable as the city prepared for its centennial bash. Never have the people of Vancouver worked with such vigour and passion to welcome the world. Our exuberance is visible. Just turn the pages and see.

Vicki Gabereau/CBC Radio Host

Lloyd Sutton

This Book is dedicated
to Charles Bellamy,
Al Graves,
and Jesse Claman

First published 1986
by William Collins Sons & Co.
(Canada) Ltd.
100 Lesmill Road, Toronto, Ontario

Canadian Cataloguing in Publication
Data

Sutherland, Tom.
Vancouver, a year in motion

ISBN 0-00-217645-9

1. Vancouver (B.C.)-Description-Views.
I. Bellamy, Cindy. II. Title.

FC3847.37. S87 1986
917.11 ' 33 ' 00222 C86-093192-7
F1089.5.V22S87 1986

Produced and Directed by
Tom Sutherland
Cindy Bellamy

Project Manager and Art Director
Leslie Smolan

Printed in Japan

10   9   8   7   6   5   4   3   2   1

Vancouver:
A Year in Motion

*A Photographic Portrait of Vancouver in
Celebration of its Centennial Year*

Collins Toronto

Vancouver is truly a city of contrasts and surprises. Magnificent natural beauty and man-made structures complement one another. Diverse nationalities maintain their identities yet join together to create the city's clear sense of community. The sights, sounds, and rhythms of the city appeal to the soul and satisfy the senses. Walk around the city's streets long enough, and the impact of its variety, from residential dwellings to skyscrapers, parks to harbour, will fill you with wonder and delight.

Present in all quarters is the urge to strut for the world, to throw back the shoulders, pound the chest and say, "Look at this place, look at the potential." On the eve of its 100th birthday, and

in anticipation of a jubilant celebration of Expo 86, Vancouver has
a renewed and justified sense
of pride.

The downtown core bubbles
with the vitality of someone on
the verge of his prime. Vancouver
is an up-and-comer with all the
right moves, a brash young urban
entity swaggering into international markets as diverse as pop
music and venture capital.

This energy travels to outly-
ing areas, enlivens the suburbs,
and sweeps back into the city like
a bracing gust of country air.

Part of the city's abundant
energy is channelled into celebration and festival. Vancouver
celebrates its waterfront with
the Sea Festival, its youth with
the Children's Festival, its
Mediterranean heritage with
Greek and Italian Days, and its
eccentricity with the Polar
Bear Swim.

Vancouverites may travel
from their city to points east or

south, seeking bigger centres with different cultural offerings or more worldly attitudes, but Vancouver's natural beauty, offspeed pace and open-collared West Coast approach to life stay with them and beckon them back.

There are few cities that can lay claim to the recreational boast of servicing skier and sailor, tennis player and hang glider all in the same day, all within 30 minutes of City Hall. Professional sports and sports enthusiasts are also attracted to Vancouver. This year, 127 world-class bicyclists came to

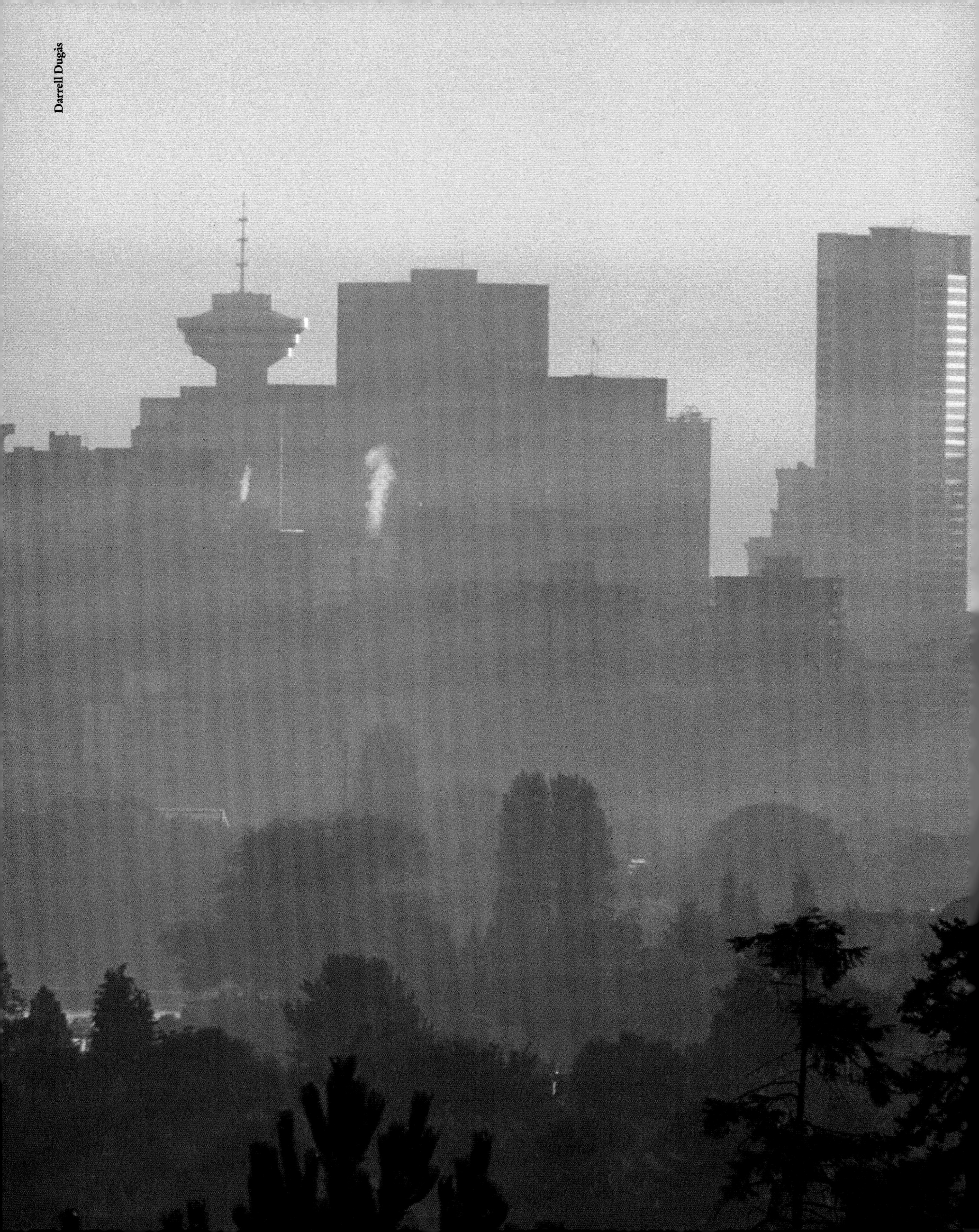

Darrell Dugas

compete in Vancouver's Gastown
Grand Prix race, and the B.C.
Lions won the prized Grey Cup,
which is Canada's most coveted
football prize.

Even fewer cities can lay claim
to a 400-hectare park, much of it
virgin timber, replete with zoo,
aquarium, and itinerant populations, both animal and human,
all within walking distance of
downtown.

From the prime industries of
forestry and fishing to the cultural
attractions of dance and theatre,
Vancouver provides all that anyone could desire in a place to live
or visit.

The purpose of this book,
then, is to present a visual portrait

January 1, 1985

January 2
*For Vancouver, 1985 arrived and departed
shrouded in fog. In January, the
city spent 21 days fog-bound, a record for
that month.*

In January, with resolutions as new as fresh layers of snow, Vancouverites took to the outdoors for recreational play. Three local mountains, Grouse, Seymour, and Cypress, all within a 40-minute drive from downtown Vancouver, provide good-quality novice and intermediate day and night skiing. For more exciting post-Christmas thrills, the world-class Whistler-Blackcomb ski runs are only an hour and a half away.

Stuart McCall

January 8
The North Shore's most famous twin peaks were originally dubbed "Sheba's Paps," then changed to the more respectable "The Sisters," and finally tamed down to "The Lions" in 1890.

The colourful shop-front window of Tony's Market reflects the ethnic influence and diversity of Vancouver. Always jammed to overflowing with delicious-looking meats, cheeses, and other delicacies, Tony's and countless other small shops along Vancouver's Commercial Drive serve the Italian community.

Activity along the 14-block span of Commercial Drive from Venables Street to Sixth Avenue reaches its high point in early July, when the street mounts a full-scale celebration. Shops display their wares on street fronts. Charcoal-grilled sausages and other meats entice pedestrians at every corner. Homemade wine is served up in highball glasses.

Everywhere one enjoys the sound of accordion music, the salute of Italian toasts, and the infectious warmth of people having a good time. Like its Greek Days counterpart, the day-long festival celebrates one ethnic group's contribution to the diverse social life of Vancouver.

Dave Kiez

January 14

*The city of Vancouver is
the result of the decision in 1884 to make
Burrard Inlet the Canadian Pacific
Railway's western terminus. With the completion of
the Panama Canal in 1914,
Vancouver has become the world's most
important wheat port, with an approxi-
mate 10,887,000 tonnes
shipped annually.*

Canada

From the lofty headquarters of *Vancouver: A Year in Motion*, photographer Tom Sutherland captures the spectacular marriage of man and nature that initially inspired him to document the city. Besides its often dramatic beauty, the Port of Vancouver is distinguished by its year-round accessibility. While the waters of many eastern Canadian ports freeze over during the winter months, Vancouver remains ice-free.

The Port of Vancouver has become the busiest port on the Pacific coast of the Americas, servicing approximately 3,000 vessels from more than 50 different countries annually. Eight ocean-going freighters arrive and depart from the port each day.

Colin Savage

January 19
*Weather officials have determined Vancouver to be
in a 17-year cycle of light to heavy snowfalls.*

Duncan Stacey/Industrial Historian

Fishing

British Columbia's fishing industry lands 10 percent of Canada's annual catch of fish, but accounts for nearly 30 percent of the monetary value of the country's fishing industry. The reason is that the 17,000 fishermen who catch the fish, the 500 tendermen who transport it, and the 7,000 shoreworkers who process it handle the highly profitable salmon and herring. More than 5,000 boats fish the five species of salmon and herring found locally. Ninety-five percent of all Canadian salmon and 59 percent of the country's herring come from British Columbia.

The Vancouver lower mainland area lands, processes, and transships most of the province's fishery products. The Fraser River was the birthplace of the province's salmon-canning industry. The area's first cannery was established in 1871 and canned salmon was exported in windjammers to Europe via Cape Horn. By 1901 more than 50 plants were in operation. Today only a fraction of these canneries is still operating.

Vancouver's first fish processing plant was a reduction operation for salmon and herring oil. Built in 1878 and owned by Joseph Spratt, it was situated on a scow and popularly known as "Spratt's Ark." Vancouver has been a major center for fresh and frozen fish since the late 1880s. A processing technology based on mechanical refrigeration either freezes the fish or produces ice in which fresh fish is transported to market. Fresh or frozen salmon

commands a higher market price than canned salmon, and once refrigeration technology became available, markets opened up for halibut and groundfish, fish that were never canned. The arrival of the Canadian Pacific Railway in Vancouver in 1887 provided direct access to the markets of Toronto, Montreal, Boston, Chicago, and New York. By 1895, B.C. was exporting 1.25 million pounds of fresh and frozen salmon and 2 million pounds of fresh halibut, a drop in the bucket compared with the 28 million pounds of canned salmon that were leaving the province. Today, however, approximately half of B.C.'s salmon is canned and half is sold fresh or frozen.

In 1906, the Canadian Fishing Company was founded at the foot of Gore Avenue on the Vancouver waterfront. This plant is still standing and can be seen from Canada Place. From the beginning it has been one of the province's largest fresh fish producers. It still has the largest cold storage and refrigeration plant on the Pacific coast, with enough room for 6 million pounds of fish.

Over the past hundred years, fishing in the province has evolved from a manual to a highly mechanized industry. The Chinese butchering gangs have been supplanted

Workers at Vancouver's Albion Fish processing plant hand-peel a harvest of fresh shrimp. An average of $20 million is generated through the harvest of shrimp and other shellfish in British Columbia.

by automation, and the Scottish
who hand gutted herring have b
by herring-gibbing machines. A
can-making, weighing, skinning
machines have mechanized the p
dustry. At sea, the backbreaking
pulling the nets is now done by
and reels. Improved refrigeration
aboard fishing and tender boats
proved the quality of the produc
couver at its centre, Canada's fis
try has become one of the finest
efficient in the world.

*A flourishing number of city restaurants,
such as this North Vancouver
landmark, have the good fortune to be within
fishing pole distance of one
of the world's richest coastal fisheries.*

Darrell Dugas

February 1
Kitsilano Beach Park becomes a winter wonderland
during a rare snowstorm.
Momentarily at rest and bathed in an unearthly glow,
swings and seesaws stand
in silent salute to the soft skyline beyond.

February 2

Over 17,000 people per month visit the Vancouver
Art Gallery to see the works of art
drawn from its $15 million collection. In 1983,
the gallery moved to its
present location in the city's old courthouse.

Cross-country skiers about to descend Mount Seymour's west slope, which is 16 kilometres from downtown Vancouver.

Mount Seymour, one of the Lower Mainland's oldest provincial parks, was opened in January 1936. A road to its 1,020-metre plateau was constructed in the early '50s, and the mountain's ski facilities came under private ownership in 1984. The new owners, Mount Seymour Ski Resorts Ltd., have since poured close to $1 million into upgrading what has always been Vancouver's family ski mountain.

An average annual snowfall of 406 centimetres falls on the mountain, which has a summit of 1,373 metres above sea level. Slopes are 90 percent novice and intermediate, 10 percent expert.

Tom Sutherland

February 6
Members of the Vancouver Parks Board battle the snow by scattering salt on the 12.8 kilometres of road around Stanley Park.

Tugboat skipper Bob Hunt smiles in the face of cold weather. On this day, the temperature fell below freezing and jammed the Fraser River with ice.

RED FIR 15

Don Whiteley/Vancouver Sun, Forestry Writer

Forestry

In 1899, Theodore Turnbull Ludgate, president of Vancouver Lumber Company, tried without success to build a sawmill near Stanley Park. While as many as five logging companies had been active in the area in the 1860s, the creation of Stanley Park in 1888 put an end to their use of that land for forestry.

In the 20th century, Vancouver has grown and prospered on the back of the very industry it once tried to keep from its doorstep. As Canada's largest port, Vancouver is a funnel for lumber, pulp and paper, newsprint, plywood, and a host of other forest products on their way to exotic places. In 1985, ships carried more than six million tonnes of those commodities to Japan, Korea, China, Germany, France, England, Italy, and the United States.

Today, forestry is by far the largest industry provincially and nationally. In 1985,

Three men guide a cargo of lumber to a waiting ship. The Port of Vancouver loads close to 2 million tonnes of lumber annually.

John Bartosik

Canada produced $25 billion worth of forest products, employed 262,226 people in making them, and paid those employees $6.4 billion in wages. Among the ten provinces, British Columbia is the leading producer of lumber in Canada, with an output in 1985 of 13.8 billion board feet, 63 percent of the Canadian total. Vancouver has become the headquarters for Canada's largest forest products companies, such as MacMillan Bloedel Ltd. and Canadian Forest Products.

The industry has not been trouble-free, however. Much wood has been harvested but,

The city's harbour waters are an essential component of the British Columbian lumber trade. Logs are boomed in water because it is a cheap form of transportation and helps prevent wood shrinkage.

Dave Kiez

until recently, very little has been replanted. And the business has been mired in recession since 1982; though production numbers are still high, 1985 will not be considered a good year because too many mills shut down, too many companies lost money, and unemployment in the industry exceeded 25 percent. Native and environmental groups are staking their claims to forests that corporations want to harvest. Under these pressures, Vancouver and the industry that built it look cautiously to the future.

Tom Sutherland

Loggers are more than rough-hewn back-woods brawlers. Trees to them are raw material for expression.

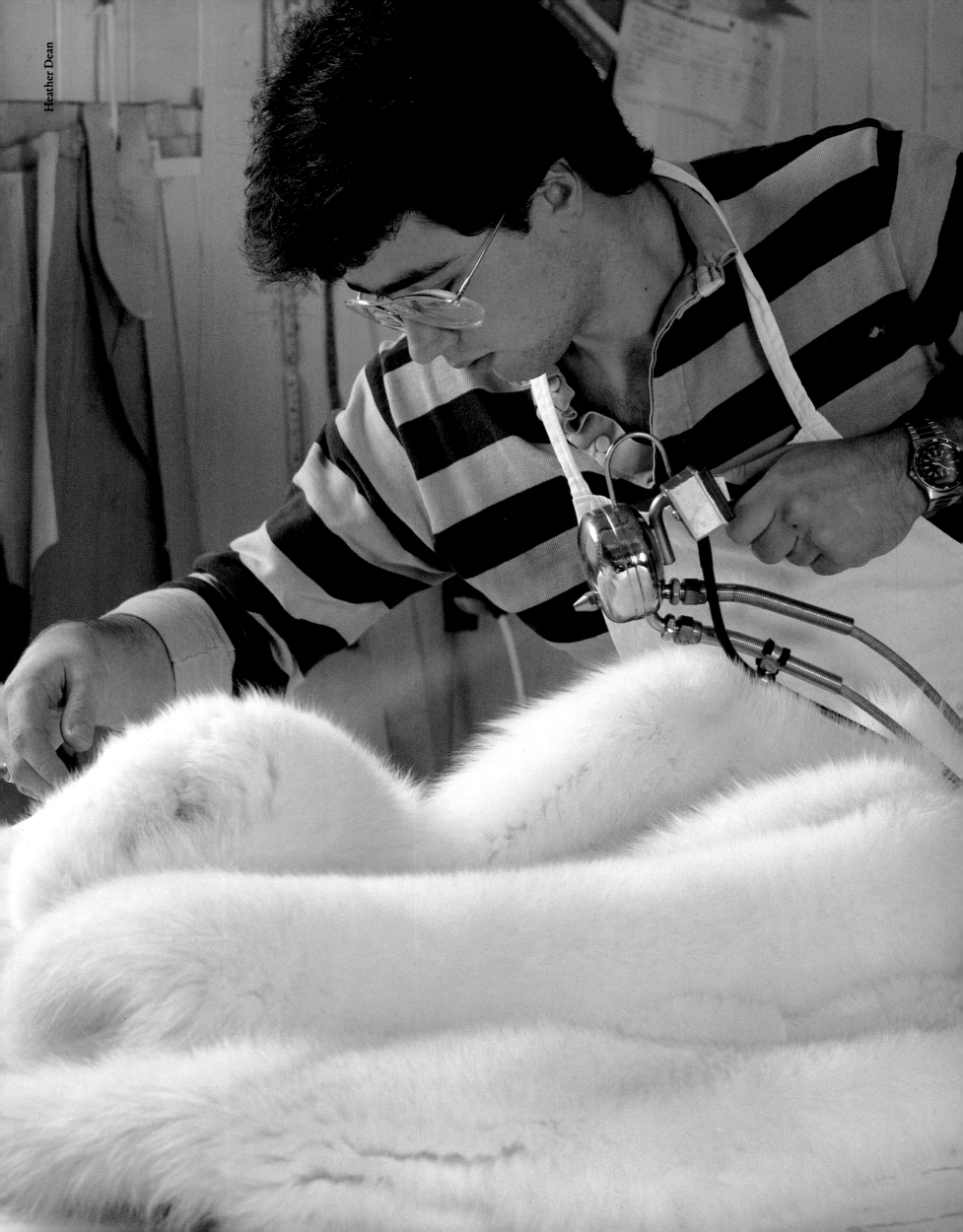

Vancouver owes its international reputation as a fur capital almost entirely to Pappas Furs. Founded in 1931, the company has grown to become the largest independent fur dealer in western North America, with annual sales in excess of $15 million. Its impressive inventory, ranging from a simple blue fox jacket ($1,000) to an opulent Russian lynx belly coat ($200,000), attracts such customers as the Prince of Saudi Arabia, the wife of Aga Khan, and Sylvester Stallone.

Company founder Ted Pappas immigrated to Canada from his native Greece in 1913. He moved to Vancouver in 1931 and opened Pappas Furs. Today, under the direction of Pappas's son Ted and grandson Constantine, the business continues to boom.

March 5
Shipments through the Port of Vancouver of such bulk commodities as sulphur increased significantly in the years following the Second World War. With close to 5,600,000 tonnes now processed through the port, sulphur currently ranks third after coal and grain shipped.

Stephe Tate

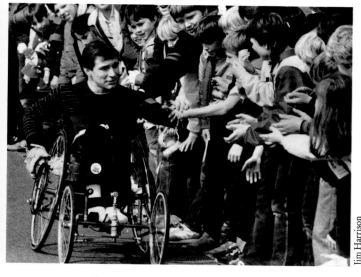

Jim Harrison

March 21
In the tradition of Terry Fox, Rick Hansen wheels into the opening day of his 40,000-km Man-In-Motion World Tour to raise money for spinal cord research. By late 1985, he had wheeled 19,024 kilometres and raised $638,000.

March 12
*Sulphur, one of British Columbia's
natural resources, provides an unusual landscape
for photographer Albert Chin.*

Albert Chin

On March 16, the
Courtenay Scottish Regiment
Seaforth Highlanders of Canada
marched away with the trophy for
Top Drill Team at the regional
military drill competition held annually at Vancouver's Seaforth Armoury. The Highlanders have
won more honours than any other
Vancouver military unit.

The Armoury, opened in 1936
by Governor General Lord
Tweedsmuir as part of the city's
Golden Jubilee celebrations, is a
Gothic, castlelike structure which
sits on the south end of the Burrard Street Bridge.

Paul Yee/Vancouver City Archivist

Chinatown

Non-Chinese envision dim-sum, firecrackers, and lion dances of the lunar New Year. They come to look, shop, and fill their stomachs just like Chinese Canadians. But stand back from the crowds and Chinatown holds more than tangy aromas and exotic colours.

The entrepreneurial drive of recent immigrants has brought new stores and offices to the area. Grocers hawk their fresh produce. New buildings are being built and old ones renovated. Commercial Chinatown is steadily pushing its boundaries outward.

Vancouver's Chinatown isn't Canada's oldest, nor is it the country's largest. It does possess, however, a strong and vital sense of the past and the future. Balconies and windows along Pender Street have witnessed a hundred years of fiery community life.

In 1907 anti-Asian mobs rampaged through the neighbourhood. Thirty years later, the Chinese Carnival erected a towering archway and pagoda for the city's 50th birthday. Noisy victory parades clogged the street to celebrate V-J Day and to mark the opening of the Chinese Cultural Centre in 1980.

Today, the vast majority of Vancouver's Chinese live outside Chinatown. They buy their fresh barbecued meats in the suburbs. They go to Chinese movies on Broadway. They can sit down to dim-sum or hot and sour soup at any number of good restaurants throughout the city.

But Chinatown remains the focal point of the community. It's a diverse community that

On February 24, the annual
Chinese New Year parade marches through
the spirited heart of
Canada's second largest Chinese community.

includes fourth-generation, Canadian-born Orientals who speak no Chinese, Vietnamese Chinese who speak no Cantonese, and recent immigrants who speak no English. What makes them a community is their shared identification with the world's oldest civilization. Parents encourage their children to speak Chinese and welcome Chinese television programming as well as Chinese videos and cassettes from Hong Kong.

They'll be proud of the classical Chinese garden being developed in the historic heart of Chinatown. Fifty Chinese artisans came here with techniques and tools perfected over the centuries in their native land. The garden will be an authentic piece of the Old World in the new.

The future? The Chinese Cultural Centre is planning to run dragon-boat races after Expo as an annual competition. New exhibition and performing arts space will become available with the completion of the Centre's multi-purpose hall. Some people want to keep the old traditions, others hope to achieve a new cultural sensibility that combines both Chinese and Canadian roots. In either case, the community will grow, its hopes and ambitions will blossom, and its energy for new projects will always focus on Chinatown.

Orange banners announcing the ceremonial twinning of Vancouver with Canton, China, hang from Chinatown's Chinese Benevolent Association building.

Kharen Hill

Lloyd Sutton

The traditional lion dance of the Chinese New Year takes place on the first weekend after

March 17

Cradled by the coastal mountain range in Golden
Ears Provincial Park, this
Boundary Bay farm is one of over 1,400 in the
Greater Vancouver Regional District.

In April, when the upper cushion of snow on the city's local mountains has receded with the coming of mild spring weather, skiers swap boots and poles for tanning salves. Cypress Mountain, because of its easy access by car and full western exposure, is Vancouver's favourite high-altitude open-air tanning spa.

For the veteran slope-side tanner, an ideal day starts with a tanning pit dug into the snow on the upper side of the Cypress Mountain road. Distance up the slope depends on personal privacy requirements versus the best location for tossing snowballs at passing cars.

Peter Dancs

April 12
*A suburb of Vancouver, White Rock
was named after a large rock deposited during the
last Ice Age and which more recently
was painted white to serve as a navigational aid.*

Expo photographer Stirling Ward captured one of the pavilion spray-painters on the site at the end of a day's work. Covered from head to toe in white paint, he flashed a smile indicative of the mood of everyone who has found employment at Expo 86.

Based on an expected attendance of 15 million people, Expo 86 will provide 53,400 person-years of employment, 18,500 of them in construction. For the construction industry, that adds up to 9,250 full-time jobs for two years.

Expo 86 expects to generate $1.08 billion in wages. The fair has an $802 million budget and Expo officials estimate that it will generate nearly $3 billion of new economic activity in British Columbia.

Darrell Dugas

April 26
Built at a cost of $126 million, B.C. Place Stadium seats 60,000 and has the largest air-supported dome in the world. The teflon-coated fibreglass roof covers four hectares, weighs 46 tonnes, and is stronger than steel.

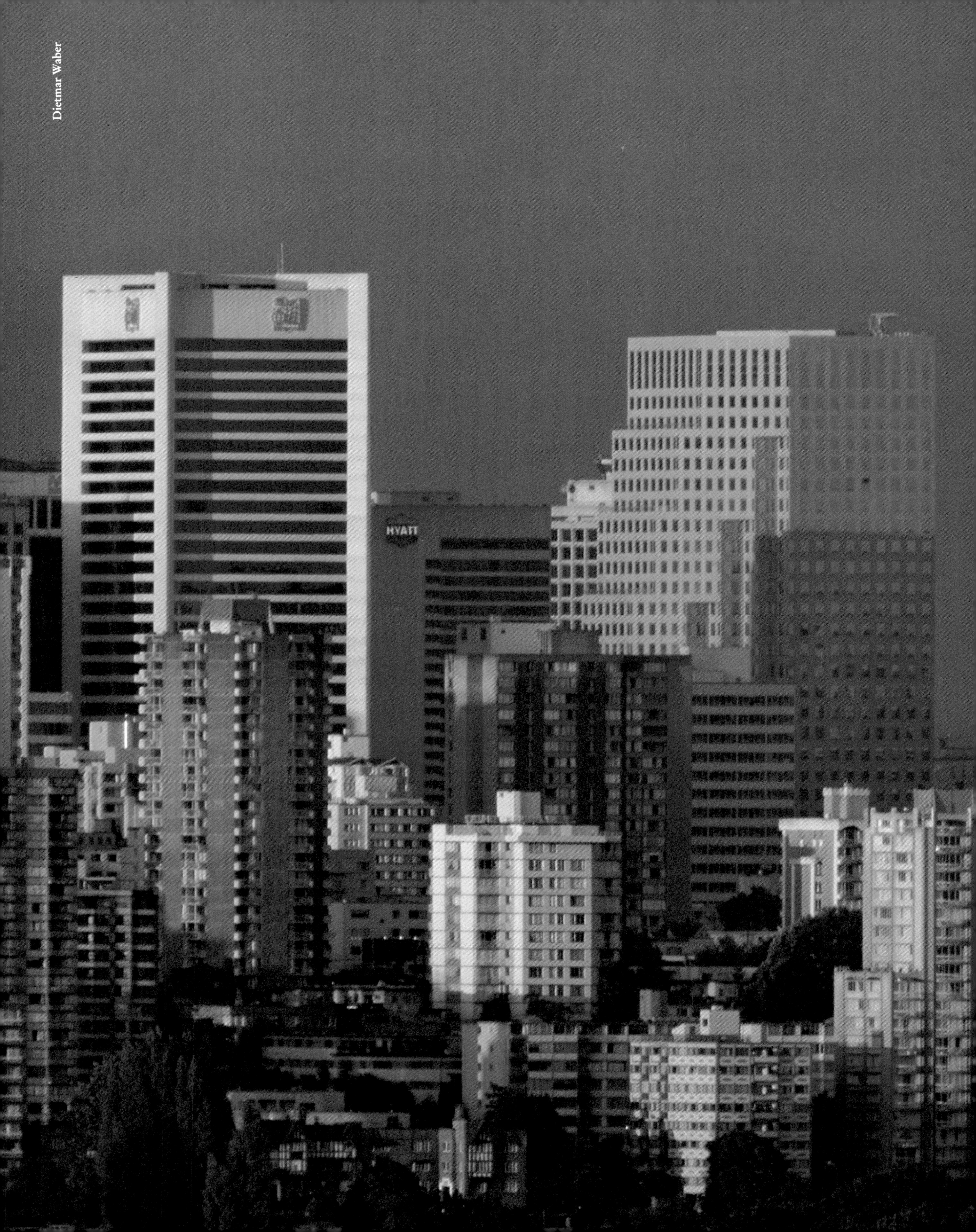

Dietmar Waber

April 28
Hotel Vancouver's green-tinged copper roof stands amidst the jungle of downtown bank towers and the recent growth of hotel competition.

Vancouver's cultural awakening was most visible in the city's vibrant young art community in 1985. During the summer, the Vancouver Art Gallery presented an exhibition of works by local artists including Philippe Raphanel, Angela Grossmann, and Derek Root (right) of the arts collective Futura Bold. Vancouver Art Gallery curator Scott Watson described this local group of artists as "the young romantics," with a bold, dramatic style.

Stuart McCall

April 29
The Emily Carr College of Art and Design moved to Granville Island in May 1980. The college currently has an enrollment of 600 day students and offers courses that include printing, painting, ceramics, sculpture, graphics, and photography.

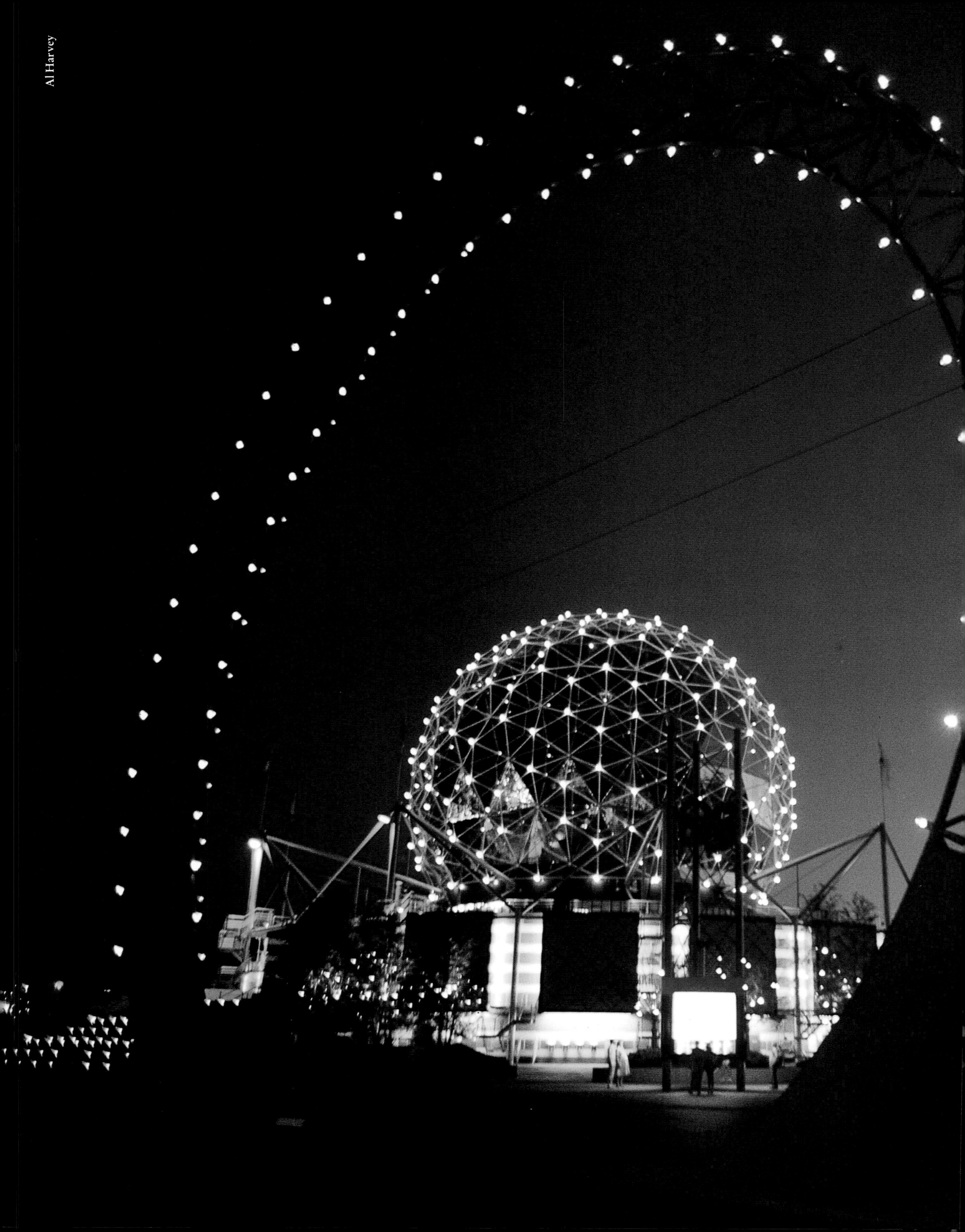

Al Harvey

Carole Taylor/"Inside Expo," Host

Expo 86

No one can doubt the splendid reality of May 1986: voices are raised in song, firework flowers fill the sky, and the Prince and Princess of Wales look on. What an opening, what a show!

But how many people remember that cold grey morning in October 1982 when the ground was broken for Transpo 86 by Premier Bill Bennett, Human Resources Minister Grace McCarthy, and Expo 86 Chairman Jimmy Pattison? The original idea was to hold a world exposition as part of Vancouver's Centennial celebrations, but there were many cynics, few believers.

Planning for Expo began with the arrival of truckloads of fully grown, blooming trees. Odd-looking buildings started to take shape, and colour, colour was everywhere. Slowly the people of Vancouver began to take notice. What was that 60-metre-high piece of wood angled so precariously by the Georgia Viaduct, anyway? A hockey stick, you say? And that glittering golf ball designed by Bruno Freschi—was that simply a temporary structure to shelter workers? No, fortunately; it was the Preview Center, our private peek at some of the intriguing surprises that awaited the people of British Columbia at Expo. But as it turned out, nearly 700,000 people visited the Expo preview.

The public's enthusiastic response to the preview was matched by the response of potential participants in Expo. More than 50

countries decided to exhibit their involvement
in transportation and communication, the
largest participation ever by countries in a
special category world exposition. This is also
the first Expo to include the United States,
the U.S.S.R., and the Republic of China. Visitors to Expo will be able to smoke a real
Havana cigar, ride on the new Japanese high-
speed magnetic levitation train, enjoy the
Kirov Ballet, watch the famous RCMP Musical
Ride, step into a real space lab, and ride on
the Scream Machine, if they dare.

Over the 165 days of Expo, there will be
14 specialized themes, each concentrating on a

*By mid-1985, the various colours
of the rapidly growing Expo 86 promotional jungle
were reaching early bloom.*

Brian Stablyk

*Expo 86's 10-train, 9-car
monorail cost approximately $15.5 million. With
99 seats per train, the system
can transport 70,000 people per day around its
5.4 kilometre Expo site track.*

EXPO
86

different aspect of transportation or communication. But all does not focus on state-of-the-art technology. The first-ever World Skateboard Championship is planned, as is a $250,000 Innovative Vehicle Design Competition. And visitors will be able to partake of the ultimate in Canadian hospitality, the Canada Place pavilion and hotel.

The year 1985, then, was a time for planning and hard work. By 1986 it was obvious to everyone that Vancouver was about to throw one terrific party.

Heather Dean

The $25 million Preview Centre opened May 2, 1985.
The 17-story geodesic dome proved so
popular that, by August 30,
it had been visited by half a million people.

A scale model of the 66-hectare Expo 86 site
as it appears in the Preview Centre.

Marin Petkov

75

May 2
From atop Burnaby Mountain,
the dominant green and blue of Vancouver's natural
surroundings are broken by
a single sailboat bound east up Burrard Inlet
towards Indian Arm.

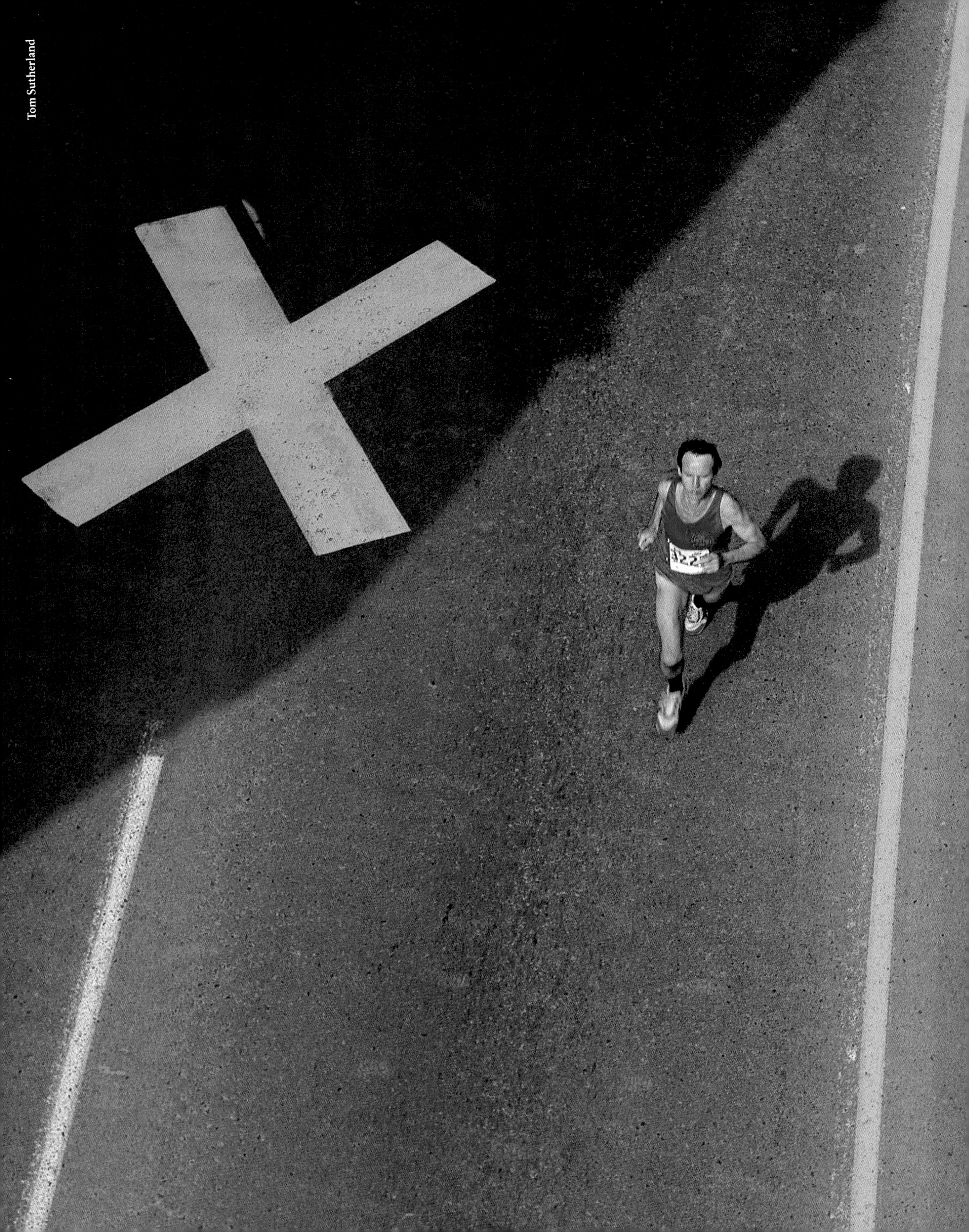

Tom Sutherland

On May 5 a runner finds himself momentarily separated from the pack in Vancouver's 14th Annual International Marathon. Fifteen hundred runners competed in the 1985 running of the 42-kilometre course. Adrian "Renaissance Man" Wellington, a physical education teacher and field hockey enthusiast from Australia, took first place with a time of 2:24:24.

The first Vancouver marathon was organized by the Lions Gate Roadrunners Club in 1972. There were 32 finishers. The Vancouver marathon has since attained an international reputation. In 1983, a record 2,000 runners finished the marathon.

Tom Sutherland

May 27
Steve Fonyo proves his courage and determination to complete a 7,924-kilometre, 14-month cross-Canada run and raise nearly $11 million for cancer research in the process.

Tom Sutherland

May 27
Steve Fonyo Sr. glows with paternal pride as the media surround him on his son's triumphant May 27th arrival.

Daniel Pearce is a do-it-yourselfer, a knitter of sweaters, and a sidewalk salesman. Vancouver requires all sidewalk salesmen to deal in goods that, like Pearce's blanket, are handcrafted. City inspectors make regular spot checks to maintain a high class of street vendors, who must pay $300 per year for a licence to occupy one of the city's 108 approved vending sites. By the end of 1985, 90 percent of those sites were already rented for the expected Expo bonanza.

May 4

Every spring the Vancouver Parks Board plants 90,000 tulip bulbs throughout the city, 10,000 of which are allotted to Stanley Park.

Albert Normandin

May 15

Simon Baker, member of North Vancouver's Squamish Indian tribe, is made an honorary Chief of the neighbouring Sechelt tribe. The Squamish are the largest of Vancouver's three native tribes.

Three of the seven Brockton Point totem poles in Stanley Park seem to reach out across the harbour to embrace downtown Vancouver as the sun sets. Originally carved in the 19th century on the north coast of British Columbia by the Kwakiutl and Haida Indians, these poles were brought here as part of an Indian village reconstruction that was never completed. The images on the poles serve as a memorial to people and events, recording the tribe's legends and heritage.

The art of totem pole carving in British Columbia had been on the decline until 1958, when local Indian carvers Bill Reid and Douglas Cranmer revitalized the craft by recreating totem poles for the Museum of Anthropology at the University of British Columbia in Vancouver. Both of these men contributed toward the restoration and preservation of the Stanley Park poles.

Two young enthusiastic participants sing out at Vancouver's annual Children's Festival. The celebration of youth began in 1978 and initially attracted crowds of 25,000; it has since quadrupled in size. As the biggest festival of its kind in North America, the event attracts entertainers from around the world.

The festival traditionally takes place during the first week of May on the 12-hectare site of Vanier Park. There is all manner of entertainment: music, theatre, mime, puppetry, story-telling, juggling, mask making, and face painting.

Kharen Hill

May 9
*Two young Children's Festival participants put
paint and brush to paper. Not only
for the 3- to 12-year-old set, the annual festival is
for anyone who wishes to
relive the magical memories of childhood.*

Cindy Bellamy

May 26
*Looking west from English Bay, one can see
the harbour in all its golden glory.*

Audrey Grescoe/Western Living Magazine, Associate Editor

The Harbour

In 1864 Vancouver was an infant port, whose only export was lumber, milled from the surrounding hills. Then came the transcontinental railway, and the little harbour bustled. Tea arrived from Yokohama in 1886 and was whisked eastward. Steamships from the Orient brought passengers, mail, rice, and silk. Ships arrived with building materials and left with lumber and canned salmon.

Today, the federally operated Port of Vancouver is the busiest port on the Pacific Coast of the Americas. Most of its facilities are clustered along Burrard Inlet, a sheltered, ice-free body of water. One in 10 workers in the Lower Mainland is employed in port activities or support services. In the morning, one can watch the freighter-nudging antics of the push-me pull-you supertug, star of the Cates

Stefan Schulhof

*In 1985, a record total of 184 cruise ship
sailings carried 267,472
passengers through the Port of Vancouver.*

nada Place, the federal government's sail-
ped pavilion for Expo that will become a
manent trade and convention centre.
nada Place houses the most modern cruise
facilities in the world, and also gives the
ple of Vancouver a chance to get closer to
port that has brought the world to their
res.

*The port of Vancouver now processes close to 60
million tonnes of raw
materials and other goods each year. The number
of containers loaded annually is
now approximately 160,000, with a total tonnage of 1½
million.*

Koos Dykstra

Like an aquatic ghost, a sunken vessel at the Coal Harbour Marina gives warning to weekend sailors and others with undeveloped sea legs. Coal Harbour was named by the crew of the HMS Plumper, which, in 1859, discovered veins of coal several centimetres thick skirting the harbour.

Tom Sutherland

May 24
Donnelly Rhodes, star of the CBC weekly adventure series, "Danger Bay," shares a secret moment with four-year-old Star Sutherland. A record $69 million was pumped into the B.C economy via the film industry in 1985.

93

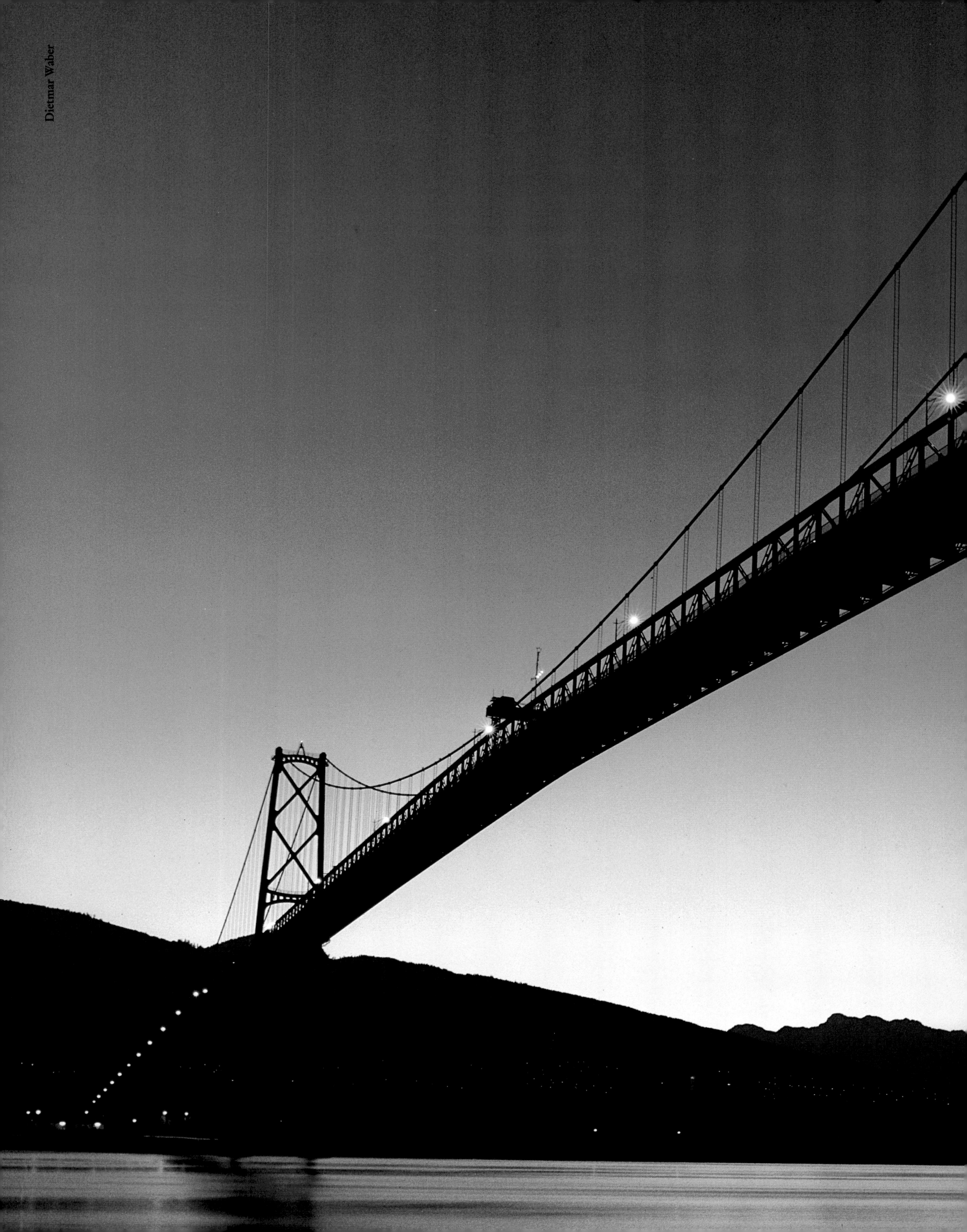

Dietmar Waber

When opened on November 12, 1938, the Lions Gate Bridge was the longest suspension bridge in the British Empire. The 2-lane, $6 million bridge was a significant event in the history of West Vancouver, for it not only helped in the development of a great new residential area, the British Properties, but it also provided easy access to downtown Vancouver. Currently 60,000 vehicles cross the bridge daily. On February 19, 1986, the Lions Gate Bridge was lit up with $690,000 worth of lighting in celebration of the Centennial and Expo 86.

95

The colourful 1985 graduation ceremony at Simon Fraser University tops off the year for 1,000 of SFU's 14,000 full- and part-time students. One of two universities in the city and one of only four in British Columbia, SFU is situated atop the 365.7-metre-high Burnaby Mountain. Since first opening its doors in 1965, the university has had a reputation for being a relatively liberal institution, its trimester system providing an alternative to the traditional academic calendar. Despite significant funding cut-backs, SFU continues to attract higher enrollments and is considered to have one of the best audio-visual facilities in Canada.

Pillars of the old Canadian Pacific Railway Station
provide convenient
leaning posts for city commuters.

Vancouver has become a city of strip show connoisseurs. The standard bump and grind will just not cut it in Vancouver. In the 20 city hotels that feature strippers (or more correctly, exotic dancers), spectators demand more elaborate entertainment. An exotic dancer in this city has to be equal parts contortionist, clown, and acrobat if she wants to stay in demand on a city circuit that boasts 400 Vancouver-based dancers.

In addition to the 20 city hotels, there are 30 suburban strip show venues. Strippers who work the Vancouver circuit can earn up to $600 per week; those who venture into the vast B.C. outback can earn double that amount, but must work harder for the money. In-town venues feature eight girls per day. Their out-of-town counterparts feature one girl all day.

Vancouver, unlike most cities, unrolls the red shag carpet for its strippers. Most clubs custom build stages for their acts, installing the poles, swings and Plexiglas showers required by the city's energetic dancers. Local strippers react to such special treatment with civic pride. At the 1984 Strippers Convention held in Las Vegas, Vancouver strippers danced off with all the top awards.

Kharen Hill

June 5
*The fourth annual Vancouver International
Film Festival rolled onto
various city screens from May 10 to June 6. A total of
160 films from 47
different countries was shown.*

Kharen Hill

Kharen Hill

June 8
*In Vancouver, as in any other city, the pursuit of
beauty is a serious business.*

June 19
The evening offshore winds of mid-June drop to a
flutter off Jericho Beach,
leaving the city's armada of windboard sailors
momentarily in the doldrums.

In the warm glow of a midsummer evening, the dance of Vancouver life shifts from a cloistered waltz to a high-stepping hoedown in Stanley Park. Square dancing, as well as classes in traditional Scottish and folk dancing, has been offered in the city's largest park for the past 30 years. With something for everyone, the outdoor dances are organized by the Vancouver Parks and Recreation Board.

June 24
*A few of West Vancouver Lawn Bowling Club's
blue-blooded members indulge in a friendly game.*

Tom Sutherland

Glen Erickson

June 4
*Kazuyoshi Akiyama, Vancouver Symphony
Orchestra musical director, raised
his baton to conduct the Vancouver Symphony
Orchestra one last time
before moving on to Syracuse, New York.*

Vancouver is a city of water. Besides its many beaches, the city has nine indoor and eight outdoor public pools. This aquatic abundance has nurtured city swimming legends such as Peter Pantages, founder of the Polar Bear Swim, and Elaine Tanner, winner of two silver medals and one bronze medal in the 1968 Olympics in Mexico City.

Kharen Hill

June 17
A monument to the city's flower-powered past, this custom-painted VW rests in the appropriate confines of a Kitsilano backyard. In the summers of love that embraced Vancouver during the late '60s and early '70s, Kitsilano was the city's "hippie haven."

During the summer of 1985, the Canada/USA "Border Wars" skateboard competition was staged in Stanley Park. On a specially constructed 3.6-metre-high vertical ramp, a total of nine professional and 14 amateur skateboarders from both countries competed for $500 in prize money. California's 17-year-old Christian Hosoi was the eventual winner.

Though there are currently 1,200 registered skateboard enthusiasts in Vancouver, facilities to practice the sport's nosedives, sweepers, aerials, and other gravity-defying stunts is are limited. The city possesses two skateboard parks, but lacks a permanent vertical ramp on which aspiring professionals can test their talent. And since Vancouverites seem to have embraced the sport with a vengeance, it may be only a matter of time until a ramp like this one is here to stay.

Kent Kallberg

June 27
*The B.C. Rugby Reps score an impressive
22-13 victory over the
touring Scottish Nationals in front of 4,000
howling rugger fans at
Stanley Park's Brockton Oval.*

Colin Savage

June 30
*Glider pilot Randy Baker practices above the North
Shore's Grouse Mountain for the World
Invitational Hang Gliding Championships. The event
attracts pilots from all over the world.*

On Canada Day, 82 male and 45 female bicyclists competed in the 13th annual Gastown Grand Prix. The July 1 race is the culmination of three events: a 15-kilometre climb up Cypress Mountain held on June 28; a 130-kilometre road race from West Vancouver to Whistler Mountain held on June 29; and a 100-kilometre Galaxy of Terror road race in North Vancouver's Deep Cove. The Grand Prix itself is a 1.3-kilometre race completed over a cobblestoned circuit with speeds often reaching 60 kph. Prize money and merchandise for the four days of racing totaled $20,000.

July 6
*If one looks east from Point Grey's
Locarno Beach, Vancouver takes on the guise of an
Australian postcard.*

Bronzed by the setting July sun, Steve Ingram takes a break from swimming laps at Kitsilano Pool. With the summer of 1985 breaking records for the number of hours of sunshine (388 in July alone), Kits Beach swimmers were out in full force. On July 2, temperatures soared to 30 degrees Celsius, a record for that day. The warm weather, although a boon to sunbathers, contributed to a larger than usual number of forest fires.

July 10
Summer sun bathes the beach-front walls of a White Rock cottage. Besides its reputation for huge tracts of sandy beach, the city is best known for its annual White Rock Sandcastle Competition.

Patrick Parenteau

Jim Harrison

July 17
Mayor Michael Harcourt takes son Justin for a swim in waters off Jericho Beach, dispelling fears that Vancouver waters are unsafe for swimming.

July 28
The $100 million, 505-room
Pan Pacific Hotel looks north over Burrard
Inlet. Behind it rises $300 million
worth of new hotels and $40 million in renovations
to existing Vancouver hotels.

Vancouver's best architects have always responded to the spectacular beauty of the city's setting and to the brooding quality of its coastal light. In its rush to greet the future, Vancouver has lost much of its past. In the 1970s, however, the designation of Chinatown and Gastown saved these historic areas of the city, while designation of heritage buildings such as the Hotel Vancouver (right), the Hudson's Bay Company Store, and the Marine Building preserved fragments of the past among the steel and glass towers of today.

The grand old Hotel Vancouver, the queen of Georgia Street, was completed in 1939. It displays the classic Gothic style of Canadian National/Canadian Pacific hotels. Because construction was stopped during the Depression, the hotel took 11 years to complete. Each room has a unique interior and the Gold Key Floor has deluxe rooms with premium service. All rooms were completely renovated in 1985 in preparation for the centennial year.

Stephe Tate

The new head-quarters for the Canadian Imperial Bank of Commerce at Burrard and Hastings streets, completed in June 1985, is typical of the many new construction projects undertaken in downtown Vancouver in that year. All over the city hoardings went up and old buildings came down to make room for new hotels, office towers, and shopping complexes, as well as the Expo 86 site. By 1986, this city had a brand new face to show the world.

Twenty-one stories high, the CIBC building was designed by the Vancouver-based Musson Kattell Mackey Partnership to complement the adjacent Daon Centre and Art Deco Marine Building. It was set back from the street to provide an unobstructed view of the waterfront and was designed to add brightness to the frequently overcast days.

Stephe Tate

Anne Petrie/CBC Broadcaster and Author

Sea Festival

During the third week of July at Vancouver's English Bay, you can catch one of the best summer festivals to be found anywhere. As dusk descends, you'll see smoke rising from the Jaycees' salmon barbecue and the silhouettes of players in the beach volleyball tournament. Overhead, skydivers dangle from parachute lines as they float to the ground. It's all part of Vancouver's oldest festival, the Sea Festival, launched in 1964 to celebrate Vancouver's aquatic history.

The festival kicks off with a colourful parade down Beach Avenue and is highlighted

Jane Weitzel

Sea Festival is the celebration of living and sailing on the West Coast. In 1985, the British Columbia Council of Yacht Clubs compiled a listing of more than 36,000 berth-nights available in the Vancouver area.

Lloyd Sutton

by a giant $500,000 fireworks display. On the third Sunday in July you can join the crowds along the sandy finish line to glimpse the winner of the Nanaimo-to-Vancouver Bathtub Race. On Kid's Day there are lots of things for the young ones to do, while on Family Day at Second Beach, all of you might enter an ice-cream-eating contest or a mini-triathlon. You can work out at the Fitness Bash, pig out at the Food Fair, or just hang out and watch the visiting naval ships. It's all part of the biggest and best party of the year.

Members of the Vancouver Fire Department struggle to win the Sea Festival tug-of-war. Despite out-muscling 20 other teams, the firemen finished second overall.

Tom Sutherland

Lloyd Sutton

This Tom Sawyer look-alike was found at one of the festival's concession stands and is one of almost 300 volunteers who gladly donate their time in order to be part of the festivities.

August 4
*Yoshimi and Terumi Ezure from Japan visit the
ninth annual Japanese Powell Street Festival,
which was begun in 1977 to celebrate the centennial
of Japanese immigration to Canada.*

126

August 8
*This pair of slobbery-chopped chaps was
photographed at West Vancouver's
Ambleside Park. In 1985, Vancouver dog lovers
purchased some 18,000 dog licences.*

KITSILANO BEACH TIDES

High .... 9:50 /4.8 Ft.
Low .... 3:45pm 4.2 Ft.
Ocean Temperature ...... 18°C/65° F.
Pool Temperature ...... 22c/76 F.

SUNDAY

AUG 4

August 4
Two lifeguards keep vigilant watch over swimmers at
Vancouver's popular Kitsilano Beach.
Originally named Greer's Beach, it was changed to the
present corrupted version of Squamish
Indian Chief Khahtsahlanough's name, which meant
"important man of the lake."

Vancouver's inhabitants retain a fascination for
the city's aquatic surroundings.
Members of the weekend fishing
fraternity commandeer boats and
take up bobbing positions at the
mouths of rivers such as the
Capilano, and cast fishing lines in
hopes of landing coho or chinook
salmon.

But a fisherman doesn't
necessarily need a boat; he can
always toss nets, cages, hooks, and
bait from the shore in hopes of
hauling in such other marine
species as cod, kelp greenlings, blue
perch, and red rock crab. No licence is required for sport crab
fishing in the Vancouver harbour,
but it is illegal to fish for crab
in False Creek, English Bay, or
between the First and Second
Narrows bridges. This restriction is mainly to ensure that nets,
lines, and traps do not cause a
navigational hazard.

Colin Savage

Gerry Kahrmann

Larry Goldstein

Gerry Kahrmann/The Province

English Bay
Beach is the centre of downtown
oceanside activity, as it has been
for the city's last 99 years.

It is where Captain George
Vancouver, for whom the city
is named, encountered a pair of
Spanish ships in the course of sur-
veying the virgin area in June
1792. It is home to major city
events, including the Sea Festival
in July and the January 1 Polar
Bear Swim, as well as the local
swimming hole for the 38,000
people who live in Vancouver's
West End.

August 30
*Bryan Adams makes his triumphant
return to Vancouver after a successful European
tour. The Vancouver rock star
won three Juno Awards in 1985 and sold over
4 million copies of his album "Reckless."*

Eleven-year-old
Gordie Maxwell cradles the neck of
his 4-H calf, Kayglen Petunia,
at the Surrey Farm Fair. A member
of the Richmond-Delta Holstein
Calf Club, Maxwell defeated 60
other entrants to win the Junior
Champion Showman title.

Surrey, which is still more
than 35 percent prime agricultural
land, is one of the fastest growing
municipalities in Canada. It now
has 165,000 people, 12 times its
population during World War II.

Tom Sutherland

August 10
*Summer recreation activities include
the traditional pursuits of
swimming and hiking as well as more unique
diversions, such as
roadside camping and dog obedience training.*

Vancouverites like to consider themselves a fashionable bunch. No longer satisfied to march to the drab rhythms of denim and pin stripes, city residents have donned attitudes more cosmopolitan and styles more daring.

In the late '60s Vancouver was home to only a handful of garment manufacturers, including Aero Garments and Original Blouse. Now Koret of Canada, Jantzen, and Britannia have set up their national head offices here, and local designers, including Christine Morton, Martha Sturdy, Zonda Nellis, Ruark Roswell, and Feizal Virani have put Vancouver on the fashion map. Taking note of the city's blossoming fashion acumen, Cartier, Gucci, and Dunhill all opened Vancouver outlets in 1985.

Cindy Bellamy

When August sunshine temporarily dispells the city's rainy reputation, even those whose fashion calls for pale skin and headdresses stake out a place in the sun. Vancouver has earned a reputation as one of the most eclectic cities in North America. Along with Los Angeles and New York, Vancouver has welcomed the subculture of wild fashion, rock and roll, slam dancing, and other punk dance steps with open arms and minds.

Stuart Dee

Patrick Parenteau

On August 31, urban artist Robert Wyland puts the finishing touches on "Orcas," the eighth in a series of whaling murals in different locations around the world. The 30.4- by 213.4-metre mural graces the east wall of a seven-story Melville Street office building, situated on the western edge of the city's financial district.

This mural is the second painted by the artist in the Vancouver area. "The Grey Whale Family," Wyland's fourth whaling wall, was a gift to the city of White Rock in 1984.

Wyland, who lives in Laguna Beach, has set out on a mission to paint 100 such walls in areas around the world noted for their offshore whale populations or their whaling industries. His aim, he says, is to bring the innate beauty of the whale to city dwellers.

September 5
*Dancer Suzanne Ouellette becomes
living art. The theatre is a
vital force in the cultural life of Vancouver with
several professional theatre groups,
three major dance companies, and over 200
professional actors.*

David Cooper

Mountain slopes
in the immediate vicinity of the city make relatively gentle demands
on residents' mountaineering
skills. For the ambitious, however,
more challenging inclines abound.
Approximately one hour by car
from downtown Vancouver,
along Highway 99, stands an im-
mense lump of granite affec-
tionately called ''The Chief'' by
local rock climbers. Its sheer face
was formed some 90 million years
ago and rises 641.4 metres to the
summit. The Chief, with three
peaks and three five-star hiking
trails, is considered ''a good
climb'' by intermediate to expert
climbers.

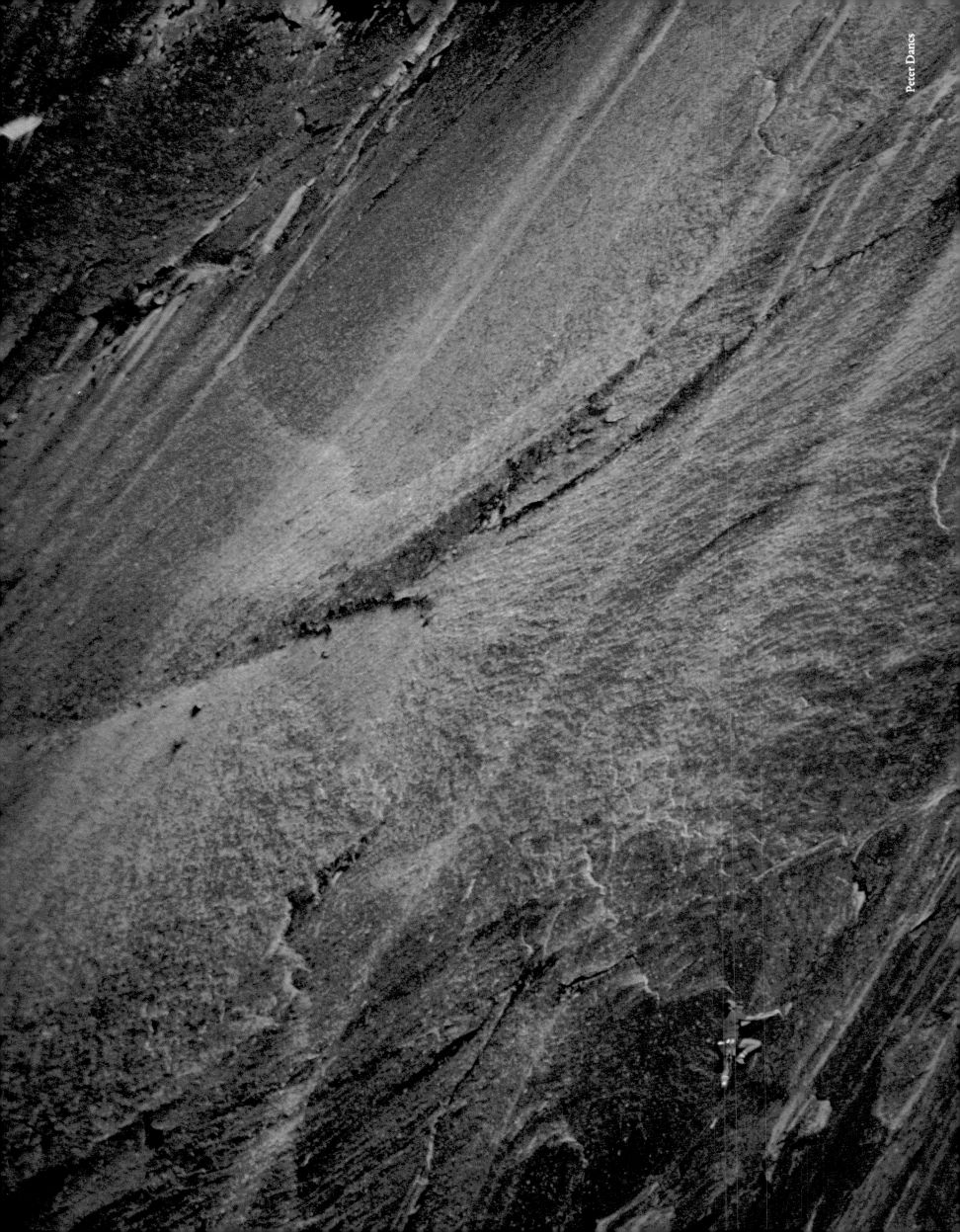

The 20-tonne image of Lord Chaitanya, the Hare Krishna spiritual leader, receives final cosmetic touches. Constructed from steel-reinforced concrete, this free-standing, 9.7-metre-high statue is supported on a single concrete foot. Construction took approximately three months at a cost of $40,000.

Followers of the Krishna faith in Vancouver have increased from two initiated members and a congregation of 10 in 1971 to 120 initiated members and a congregation of roughly 10,000 in 1985.

September 16

*In 1985, Vancouver's Exhibition Park Race Track
had an attendance of 1.1 million
people and saw 144 million in gambling dollars
flow through its gates.*

Koos Dykstra

Danny Wirth, a member of the Sunshine Band, a country and western trio, poses with Stella Schuller, the band's unofficial fan club secretary. As he has for the past 10 years, Wirth performs with two other urban cowpokes. Though cowboy traditions in Vancouver are less prominent than those of the fisherman and the logger, the music of the cowboy enjoys a small but enthusiastic local following.

September 21
A BMX bicyclist leaps across the urban backdrop of east end Vancouver. Despite its growth, the city remains a blend of the industrial, the commercial, and the recreational.

Greg Kinch

Colin Savage/The Province

September 18
Members of the Vancouver-based Greenpeace environmental group chained themselves to outflow pipes of a Fraser River paper processing plant to protest the dumping of toxic wastes.

Paul Grescoe/Communications Counsellor and Author
Stanley Park

"There are parks and there are parks," wrote distinguished American author Elbert Hubbard at the turn of the century. "But there is no park in the world that will exhaust your stock of adjectives and subdue you to silence like Stanley Park in Vancouver." The city's splendid urban preserve, which celebrates its 100th birthday in 1988, is the single tourist attraction that must be seen by visitors to Vancouver. For residents, it's a place to picnic beside a grove of totem poles, to dine on B.C. Coho and Baked Alaska, or to play cricket, soccer, rugby, tennis, or golf. It is a park for all seasons, with activities ranging from ice skating on Lost Lagoon in winter to feeding resident Canadian geese in the fall.

The Royal Engineers set aside the parkland for the government of the colony of British Columbia in 1863. In 1886, the new

Two joggers circle Stanley Park's 9-kilometre seawall. Construction was first begun on the wall in 1916 and completed 59 years later.

148

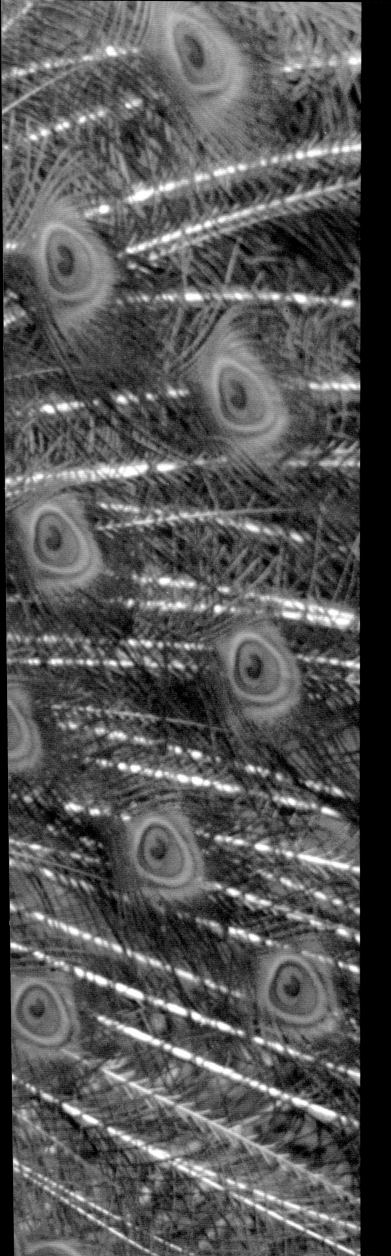

Vancouver City Council petitioned the federal government to acquire the site, and Stanley Park was first opened to the public two years later. Vancouver has had a passionate affair of the heart with the park ever since. Families sit amid the scent of cedar and Douglas fir at Theatre Under the Stars. Square dancers do-si-do in the summer twilight on Ceperley Meadow. Runners hold an annual marathon on rosebush- and tree-lined roads. Seven million people each year wander through the main zoo and the children's zoo of farm animals. The park's Vancouver Public Aquarium is Canada's largest, with more than 8,000 specimens. In honour of Expo 86, a new $5 million pool was built for the aquarium's whales.

Perry Zavitz

Celebrating its 30th anniversary in 1986, the Vancouver Aquarium has over 8,000 specimens including a five-tonne killer whale. It is the largest aquarium in Canada, and one of the top five in the world.

151

Outside the Montgomery Cafe, a young woman takes a break from the rigors of life among Vancouver's young artists and musicians. The Montgomery, once a coffee shop, has since been taken over by a more worldly management. Modern bistro cuisine, espresso coffees, and upscale hamburgers are served in an atmosphere replete with modern graphics and neon lighting. In addition to supplying sustenance to the artistically inclined and financially strapped, the Montgomery provides a showcase for new artwork.

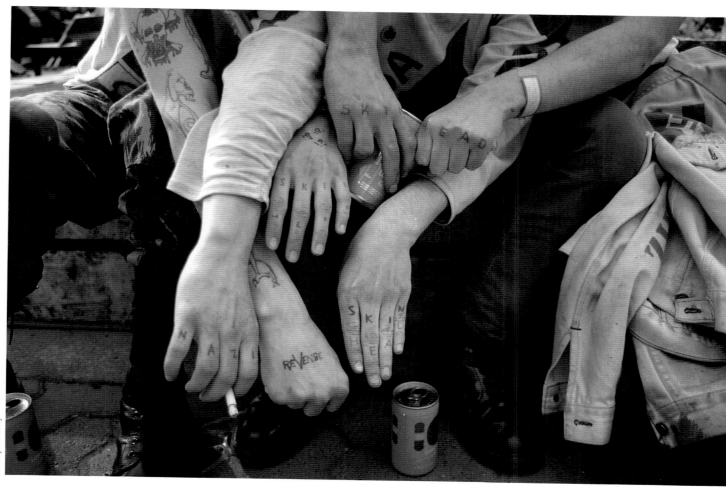

Cindy Bellamy

September 15
Vancouver has developed a penchant for the dramatic, an attraction to the extreme, and an eye for the odd.

Kharen Hill

September 28
With only four professional tattoo parlours in Vancouver, sporting such names as Mum's and the Mystic Needle, tattoo collectors in the city are a select breed.

October 24
*Under a canopy of autumn leaves, a few
of the 26,000 students
enrolled at the University of British Columbia
make their way to classes.*

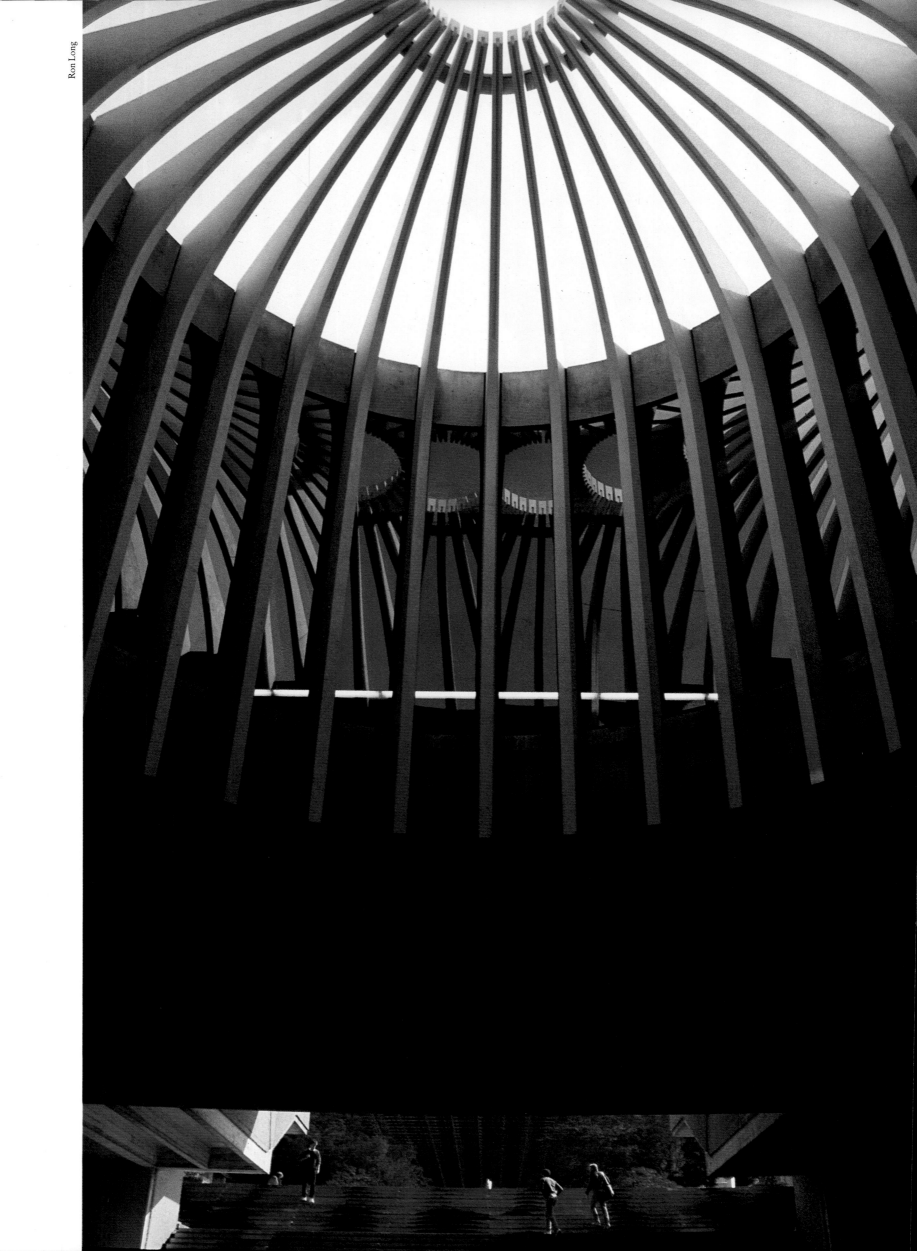

Fall colors peek through the halls of Simon Fraser University on October 7. Designed by renowned Vancouver architects Arthur Erickson and Geoffrey Massey, SFU contains a central mall bordered by five main buildings. Its futuristic design was used as the backdrop to the 1971 science fiction film, "The Groundstar Conspiracy."

October 2

North Shore commuters queue for the journey home across the Lions Gate Bridge. Completed in 1938, the $6 million three-lane wonder now carries approximately 60,000 vehicles across its span daily.

Perry Zavitz

Colin Savage

October 10

Capilano Fish Hatchery personnel attempt to net Chinook salmon at the mouth of North Vancouver's Capilano River and transport the fish to the hatchery to spawn.

The commercial success that is the city's Granville Island glows in neon beneath the sombre Granville Street Bridge.

Once an abandoned industrial site, Granville Island now attracts some six million visitors per year to its retail shops, public market, brewery, theatre, hotel, Sea Village, and numerous restaurants. It is a place for local craftspeople to make and sell their wares. As part of the government's $20-million rehabilitation effort, the island's industrial heritage has been preserved in refurbished old buildings and new ones that echo an industrial theme.

Al Harvey

October 20

Chasing the chill from a cool October evening,
a young Vancouver couple embraces
under the discreet gaze of a bus stop advertisement.

Peter Bennett

October 12

In contrast to its dilapidated look
of a few years ago, Granville Island has become
an attractive, bustling center
for business people, artists, industry,
and the public.

October 19

*The lights of Vancouver's downtown skyline dance
on Coal Harbour waters.*

Despite their fearsome appearance, the wolf eels that frequent the ocean waters around Vancouver are generally harmless. They live in rocky dens at moderate depths in the Strait of Georgia and can grow up to 2.4 metres in length.

The approximately 241 kilometres of ocean coastline and river-bank in the Greater Vancouver area provide some of the best skin-diving in the region. Two North Shore bays, Whytecliff and Telegraph Cove, form what is Canada's first undersea park.

October 24
The glory of Vancouver's marine abundance fills the shop window of West Vancouver's Royal Seafoods, now in its 24th year.

Cindy Bellamy

October 26
A candy-striped shrimp clings to a sea anemone, which, despite its stinging tentacles, provides the food scraps upon which the shrimp survives.

Great blue herons can be seen stalking fish along harbour shorelines or in lower mainland marshlands. More than 40 heron nests have been sighted in Stanley Park, unusual given the park's urban location. Even during late fall and winter months, Vancouver is alive with birds. Approximately 130 species, more than are found in any other area in Canada, take advantage of the city's unusually mild winter. In total, the Greater Vancouver area is home to some 230 species of wild birds.

Martin Roland

October 18
To protect the city's irreplaceable coastline, six oil companies developed Burrard Clean Oil Spill Cooperative, one of the West Coast's best oil spill response teams. It has attended 300 oil spills in the harbour and along the British Columbia coast since 1976.

October 31
Though Vancouverites are basically conservative,
the city's mild climate combines
in a special way with the abundance of sea air to
occasionally loosen inhibitions.

October 14
Vancouver Canuck defenceman Rick Lanz (right)
and New York Islander
centre Brent Sutter battle for the puck in a
4-2 Vancouver victory.

From November 15 to November 30, Vancouver's Tamahnous Theatre company performed Sally Clark's "The Trial" at the Vancouver East Cultural Centre. The black comedy, an interpretation of Franz Kafka's famous novel, was given an unusual twist by Ken MacDonald, co-designer for the production. MacDonald built and painted 15 plywood cartoon cutouts which were worn like sandwich boards by the six actors. The plywood cutouts, according to MacDonald, were an experimental form of set and costume design that portrayed both the two-dimensional and larger-than-life aspects of the characters in the play. Moving on and off the set in a specially choreographed sideways crab-walk to the music of Kevin Cey, they also provided a colourful contrast to the overall starkness of the set. Tamahnous was established in the early 1970s as an experimental theatre cooperative.

Albert Chin

Wayne Velestuk is the reincarnation of a breed many assumed had long since vanished. He still delivers milk door-to-door in real glass bottles. From a casual offer to deliver bottled milk to 30 households four years ago, Wayne now employs five drivers to deliver almost 6,000 litres of milk per week throughout the Greater Vancouver area. He started with an '81 Econoline van but traded it for a more authentic '64 Ford one-tonne milk truck. Besides delivering Avalon milk, Wayne's Dairy Service delivers cold Granville Island Lager, grain-fed chicken, and free-range eggs.

Dietmar Waber

November 2
*The farmlands of Richmond have
helped quench the thirsts of Vancouver milk lovers
since the 1890s, when the
municipality's Sea Island Dairy was the area's
main milk producer.*

November 13

*A shoe merchant polishes his storefront
display case in historic Gastown,
Vancouver's original town centre. Revitalized in
the late 1960s, it has become a
thriving centre of the city's tourist industry.*

By November 15, 1985, the Vancouver Stock Exchange was well on its way to achieving one of its best years ever. Trading activity was the second highest on record with 2.75 billion shares changing hands; the VSE price index rose by almost 60 percent, and monies raised by VSE companies hit a record $274.4 million, breaking the previous high of $218 million set in both 1980 and 1981.

The original VSE was incorporated on April 25, 1907. It had 12 charter members and the price of a seat on the exchange was $250. Today there are 67 seats on the VSE, one of which was sold in 1985 for $43,000.

Since its original incorporation, the VSE has moved seven times. Its latest change of address occurred in October 1981, when it moved from 536 Howe Street to its present location in the Pacific Centre, 609 Granville Street.

During the real estate boom created by Expo 86, office towers in downtown Vancouver were going up in record numbers. In 1985, more new office space was constructed than ever before, more than five times the amount built during the previous year—totaling 185,000 square metres. Some of these new buildings were Daon's Park Place, a Bank of Commerce tower, and the Texada-Simons building.

Al Harvey

November 20
In 1985, there were 91 Vancouverites licenced to sell food and knick-knacks on city streets. For chestnut vendors, winter is traditionally the high season. They make up to $8 per hour plus sales commission.

Vancouver's war veterans congregate in Victory Square on November 11 for Remembrance Day services. Many of the city's 35,000 veterans, including representatives from each branch of the Canadian Armed Forces, participate in the annual veterans' parade that culminates at Victory Square.

The Square's monument, unveiled on April 27, 1924, was erected to commemorate the veterans of the First World War. It was built on the site of the original Vancouver courthouse, which was demolished in 1981.

Dietmar Waber

November 11
A Vancouver veteran offers a private salute to his fellow soldiers who fought during the Second World War.

Since their debut in 1970, the Vancouver Canucks have achieved mixed results but always attracted a loyal following. Here photographer Derik Murray provides a bird's-eye view of the action on November 14.

November 28

When real winter weather comes to the city as it did in late 1985, Stanley Park's Lost Lagoon becomes a beautiful open-air skating arena.

Colin Savage

Anji Smith

November 27

Carmine Bernhardt takes a break from skating on the temporarily frozen Lost Lagoon, which is deemed safe for skating when its ice is at least 10 centimetres thick.

No one revels in the growing versatility and sophistication of Vancouver's restaurants more than James Barber. He is arguably the city's most influential food personality, and his endorsement is a restaurant's ticket to uptown commercial success. Dubbed "Adam in the Garden of Eating" by *Sun* columnist Denny Boyd, the bearded gourmet has written three cookbooks and starred in his own CBC-TV television show, "Midnight Snacks." In 1985, besides cooking in every major city in Canada, Barber founded the Urban Peasant Cooking School on Pender Island.

November 17
Two kitchen workers at Isadora's Cooperative Restaurant take a mid-morning break. The Granville Island restaurant opened in May 1983, selling public ownership shares at $100 each. The current 1,800 shareholders each receive an annual $25 food voucher while Isadora's profits go towards improvements, staff wages, and various community functions.

Cindy Bellamy

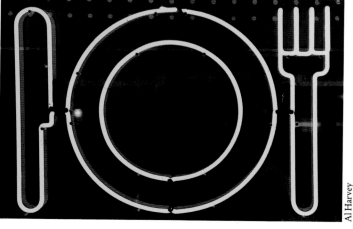

Al Harvey

November 18
Vancouver has a rich neon heritage. In the 1950s, Vancouver was second only to Shanghai, China, in neon sign footage.

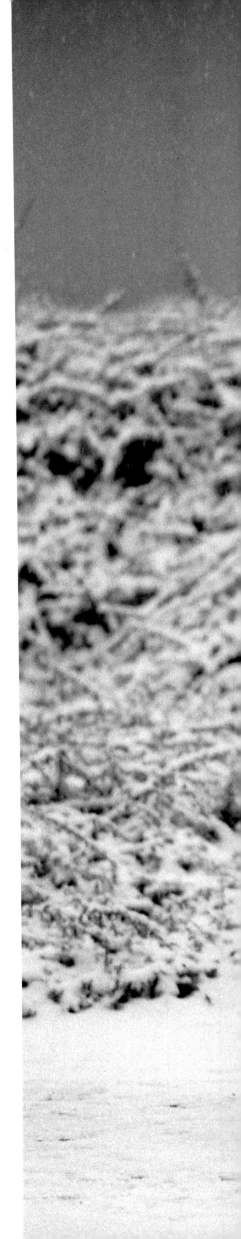

In late November, the first snowfalls of the 1985 winter season hit Vancouver with unexpected accumulations of 14.6 centimetres over a period of six days. Inhabitants, accustomed to an average November snowfall of a mere 2.8 centimetres, were delighted by this change of pace from the predictable winter rain, and dreamed of an early ski season. Unfortunately, Vancouver snow is notoriously wet, and regardless of flake size and moisture content at the outset, it quickly turns into a blanket of slush covering the city's hills and streets. This early snowfall was no exception.

Michele Smith

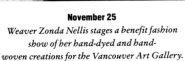

November 25
Weaver Zonda Nellis stages a benefit fashion show of her hand-dyed and hand-woven creations for the Vancouver Art Gallery.

James Lawton/Vancouver Sun, Sports Columnist

The B.C. Lions

On Hamilton's first play in the 1985 Grey Cup, running back Johnny Shepherd rambled deeply into B.C. Lions territory. Vancouver's collective heart skipped a beat in Montreal's Olympic Stadium. For 21 years the city had coveted Canada's highest football prize, the Grey Cup.

Before the game, veteran centre and team captain Al Wilson had confided that "the fear of defeat is terrible. I've been carrying it like baggage for days. For 14 years I've been striving to win this thing. I know we are the better team, but football, like life, doesn't always work out the way it should."

Wilson's worst fears went unrealized, thanks to the fierce, confident spirit of the B.C. Lions. With less than a minute showing on the clock, and with the Lions 13 points ahead, Wilson ran from the sidelines to kiss his wife. The quest was over.

In the dressing room, Lions defensive lineman Nick Hebeler poured champagne

Tom Sutherland

*Receiver Ned Armour steps into the large
shoes of injured star receiver
Mervyn "Swervin' " Fernandez and comes away with
two key Lions' touchdowns.*

Screaming fans go wild over the B.C. Lions' 42 to 22
Western Final Win

over the head of B.C. Premier Bill Bennett. Tears of emotion rolled down Wilson's face, but when the club's general manager, Bob Ackles, handed him the Grey Cup, he wiped his eyes, grinned, and said, "I'd like to see the sonofabitch who tries to take this away."

The win was a climax to years of hard work by head coach Don Matthews. When he arrived from Edmonton, Matthews inherited a talented but temperamental team. After defeats by Toronto in the 1983 Grey Cup and by Winnipeg in the 1984 Western Final, Matthews finally had the right talent and psychological combination for the big one. For Ackles, the sweetness of triumph was exquisite. He had seen the club through its financially shaky beginnings in 1954, up to the first great climax, the 1964 Grey Cup. And then came the long years of drought. During the tense days before the 1985 Grey Cup game, Ackles was plagued with insomnia. Old superstitions flared. In the elevator of the team hotel, he reached down beside a club director to pick up a dime. Ackles believed finding money before a big game was a power-

Often criticized and harshly judged, B.C. Lions head coach Don Matthews ignored the bad press, and led his team to the big one.

Kent Kallberg

The Hamilton Tiger Cats and the B.C. Lions face the game's inevitable outcome.

Al Harvey

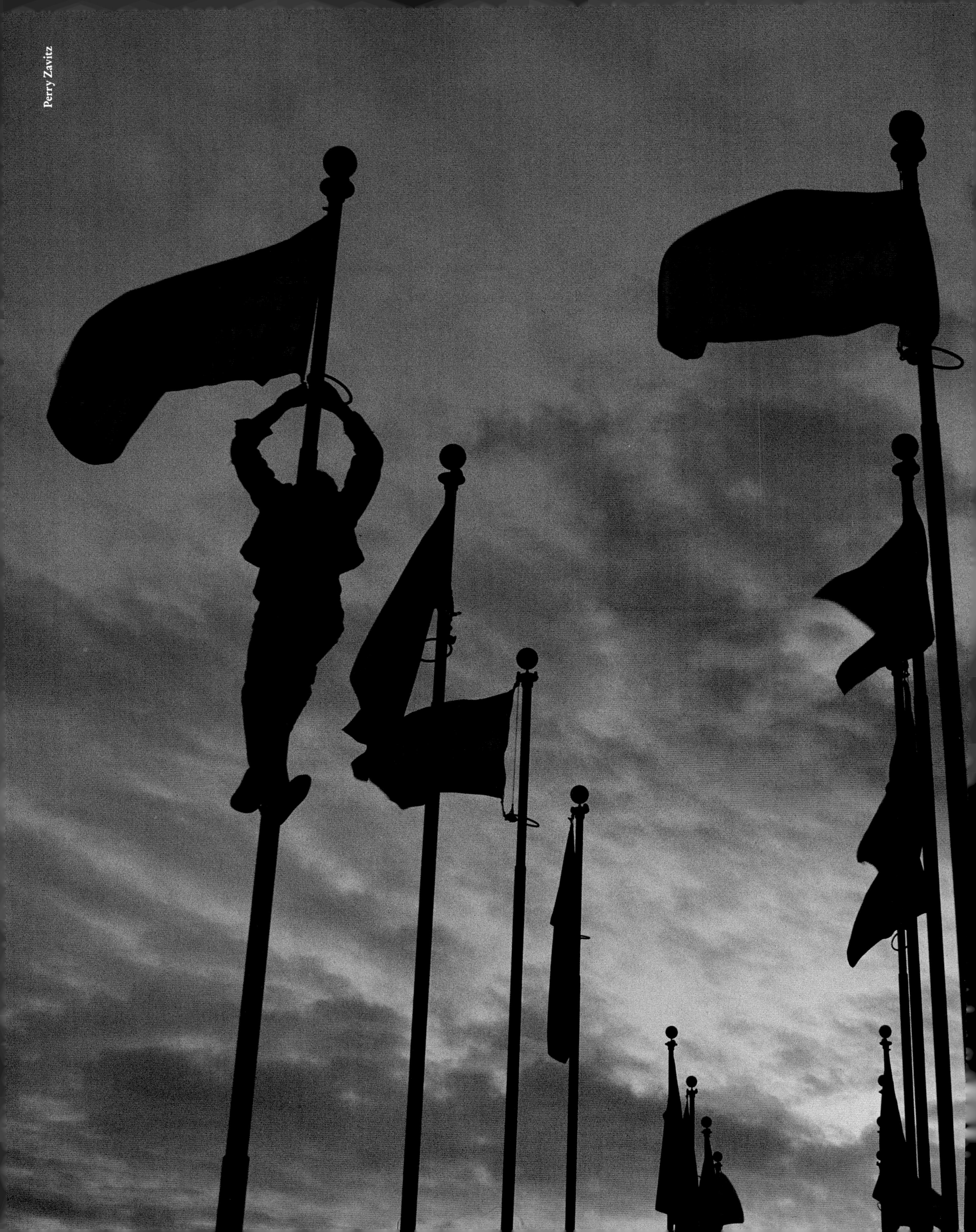

Perry Zavitz

how important this could be."

Maybe he was right. Of course, more than just luck was working for the Lions when they won the Grey Cup that cold day in Montreal. That's why the streets of Vancouver were choked with fans on the sub-zero day the Lions came home—the Lions, at last, had roared in winter.

Coach Matthews wears the ticker tape garland of honor while accepting the personal congratulations of one of Vancouver's sports fans.

Tom Sutherland

Peter Bennett

. . .for the first time in 21 years.

Kent Kallberg

Guard Glenn Leonhard (left) shares a quiet moment of locker room camaraderie with centre Al Wilson, a 14-year veteran of the B.C. Lions.

189

In the proud tradition of the Vancouver City Police Mounted Patrol, Constable Jack Emdall surveys his Stanley Park beat. Although the mounted squad was disbanded in 1949, a visit from Princess Elizabeth and Prince Philip reinstated the group two years later. Though occasionally faced with major crimes, the nine officers and 10 horses in the Squad spend the greatest portion of their time tracking down thefts from automobiles, policing beach parties, and controlling traffic.

Colin Savage

December 6
*Rupert Lang dispatches the chill
of December with a cappuccino from a West
Vancouver espresso bar.
Once a rarity in all but the ethnic ends of town,
espresso bars have invaded every
area of the city.*

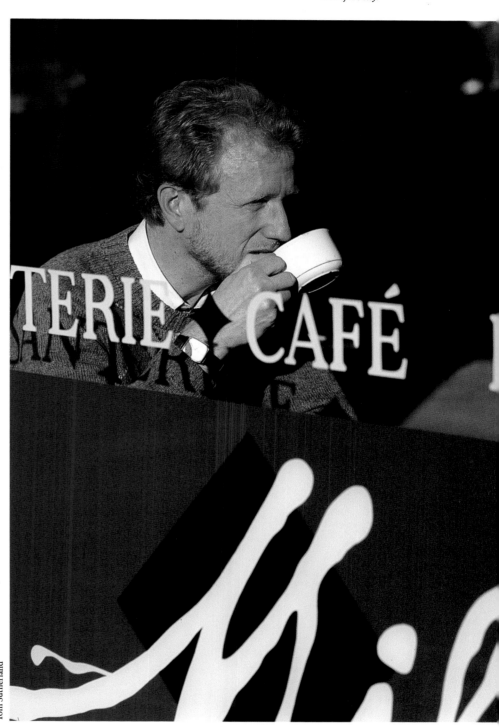

Tom Sutherland

Jim Harrison

December 9
*The Vancouver chapter of Mothers Against Drunk
Drivers (MADD) holds a candlelight
procession to focus attention on the annual highway
carnage caused by drinking drivers.*

The migration of a massive flock of snow geese from the Reifel Migratory Bird Sanctuary on December 1 signals the onset of winter. The sanctuary is a 40-hectare bird preserve located on tidal marshes at the mouth of the Fraser River's south arm. Thousands of snow geese migrate from their Arctic breeding grounds to protected waterfowl marshes in California's Sacramento River Valley. The Reifel sanctuary is one of their major ports of call en route. Flocks of up to 10,000 usually arrive in mid-November and stay approximately two weeks, feeding on grass and other available foods. The Reifel sanctuary, leased to the British Columbia Waterfowl Society in 1963 by society founder George Reifel, is approximately 45 minutes from Vancouver and boasts Canada's largest winter bird population.

Constable Leslie
Hallet during a tour of duty
on December 7. Hallet, one of 53
women now serving on the
1,045-member Vancouver Police
force, feels that things have
improved for female officers since
she first began 11 years ago. "It
was difficult at first. Women were
treated differently. Male officers
had a hard time adjusting to female
officers, and I think that the public
always felt that women were just
not as capable." Although women
first joined the Vancouver Police
Department in 1912, it was only in
1957 that they began to earn the
same wage as male officers and were
afforded the same right to compete for promotion. "Now," says
Hallet, "we are treated as compe-
tent officers. Nothing more,
nothing less."

December 15
*In order to capture the Vancouver
Police Department from a
different perspective, Constable Koos Dykstra mounted
his camera on the hood of a police
cruiser and took a midnight photographic drive
down Granville Street.*

Koos Dykstra

Jim Harrison

December 11
*Mayor Harcourt raises the
ceremonial scissors to cut the ribbon across the new
$6 million Cambie Street Bridge.
The new bridge replaces one that was built in 1911
for $740,000.*

195

Peter Bennett

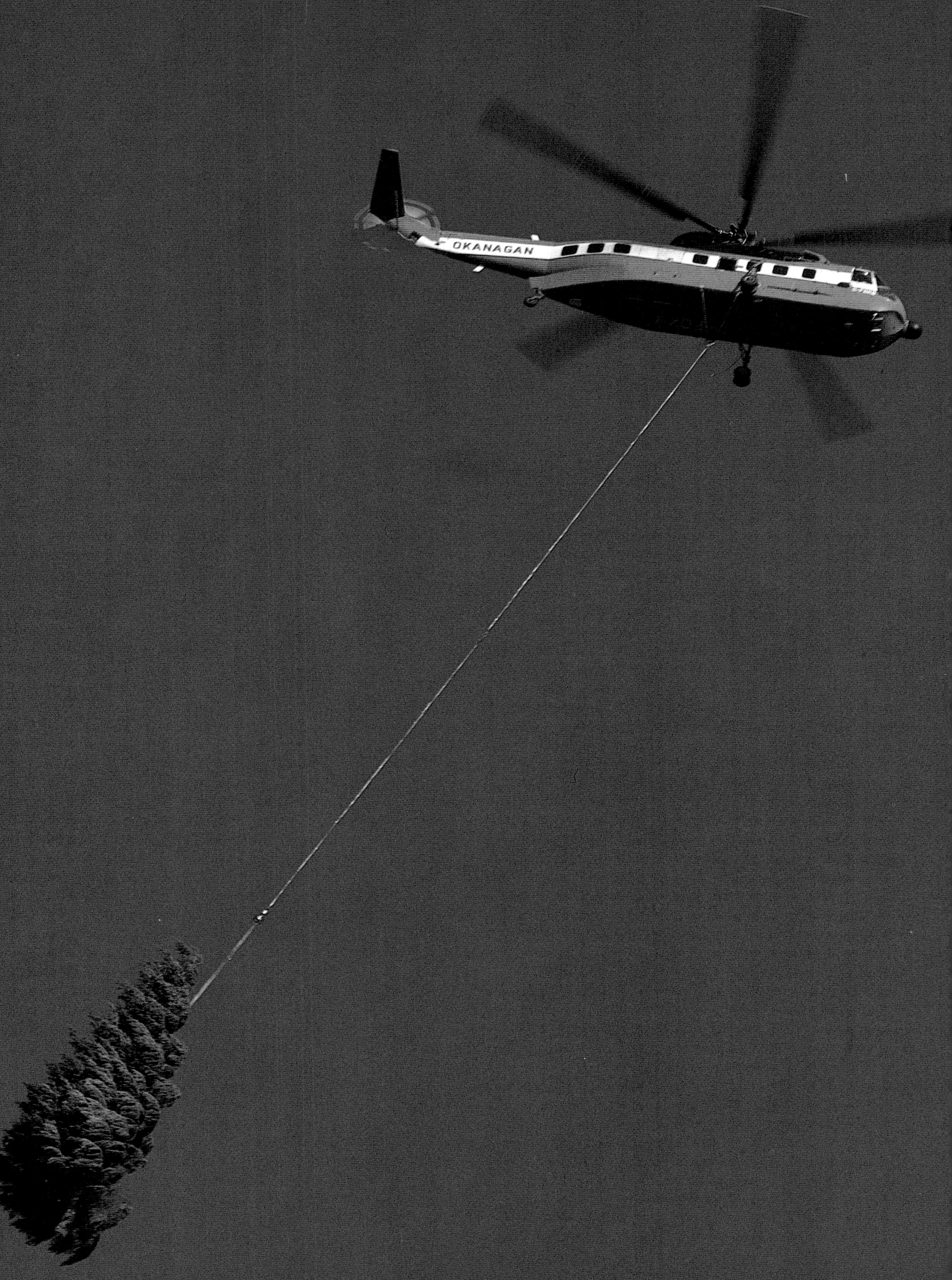

On December 8, a 12-metre Christmas tree was hauled via an F-61 Sikorsky helicopter from Sooke, B.C., to the B.C. Pavilion on the Expo site. The tree was outfitted in fully illuminated Christmas light regalia and flown over the city and its dumbfounded citizenry as a publicity stunt to help ring in the grand opening of the new Cambie Street Bridge.

Dave Kiez

December 9
*The caloric Christmas pageant of artistic
confections makes its debut
in early December. Other holiday traditions
include a harbour cruise
of gaily lit carol ships and hopes for
a white Christmas.*

December 31
*Vancouver says good-bye to 1985 in the same way it
said hello 12 months earlier—in a fog.*

With the coming of the new year, Vancouverites perform a ritual that is the city's contribution to the world roster of oddball events.

The Polar Bear Swim has, from humble beginnings, become a collective city-wide venting of suppressed urban frustrations. Peter Pantages, a Greek immigrant, founded the Polar Bear Club in 1920, one year after his arrival in Vancouver. His fanatical devotion to ocean water and its therapeutic value led him to decree that he would swim in ocean waters every day of the year. It was a self-imposed edict that he followed with only minor exception until his death in 1971 in waters off Hawaii.

His legacy is the annual January 1 plunge. From the initial six Polar Bears, the numbers have ballooned to a record 2,250 swimmers in 1983, with attendant crowds in the tens of thousands. In 1985 there were 1,890 registered Polar Bears.

Though the event has been adopted in other parts of the world, the Polar Bear Swim remains a Vancouver original.

January 1, 1986

The Centennial Year Begins

Vancouver:
A Year in Motion
Photographers and
Writers

Ken Baker

Baker travelled extensively for five years in five countries before settling in Vancouver. Baker now works as a free-lance photographer and owns a portrait studio in Vancouver.

John Bartosik

After five years of exploring and photographing the mountainous area of British Columbia, Bartosik published a book titled *Sea to Sky Country.* His photos adorn many corporate walls and have appeared in calendars, brochures, and audio-visual productions. Bartosik studied filmmaking and photography at Ryerson Polytechnic Institute in Toronto, Ont.

Les Bazso

Hungarian-born free-lance photographer Bazso moved from Ottawa to Vancouver in 1980. He has worked for various daily and weekly newspapers such as the *City of Ottawa Exposition 86,* as well as the Canadian Press and United Press Canada. He is a winner of Canadian Press Pictures of the Month awards and Canadian Weekly Newspaper Pictures of the Year awards. Bazso currently photographs for the Vancouver *Province* newspaper.

Cindy Bellamy

Bellamy is co-producer of *Vancouver: A Year in Motion.* After studying photography for three years, Bellamy decided to put her talents to use photographing the city she knows best. As the youngest photographer on the project, Bellamy's first professional effort proves a strong beginning for a new talent. Bellamy is a native of Vancouver.

Peter Bennett

Bennett's photographs and travel articles have appeared in a variety of Canadian, British, and African publications. He recently returned to Vancouver after two years of photographing throughout Africa. He currently works on editorial, audio-visual, corporate, and publishing assignments.

Barry Brooks

After graduating from York University in Toronto, Brooks travelled and worked as a free-lance photographer. His work has been shown in galleries in Toronto and Italy as well as in commercial and non-commercial publications in Canada, the United States, and Hong Kong. Assignment work for multi-image productions has also taken him to Japan, Singapore, Thailand, Australia, the U.K., and the south of France. Brooks has worked as chief photographer on several award-winning productions and recently was awarded the gold medal for best multi-image production by the International Association for Business Communicators.

Albert Chin

Chin studied photographic techniques at the University of British Columbia. His stock photos have appeared in numerous regional publications. Chin's clients include the *Expo 86 Guide Book* and *Tourism B.C.* He also does annual reports and audio-visual productions.

Wayne Chose

Chose is a professional photographer, writer, and audio-visual producer. After 15 years with MacMillan Bloedel Ltd., where he produced international and public-relations slide shows, he formed his own company, Canadian Marathon Photos. This photography and audio-visual company handles commercial, industrial, editorial, and sports photography for such clients as Imperial Oil, MacMillan Bloedel, the Y.M.C.A., Keg restaurants, Honda Canada, and Government Information Services (B.C.).

Richard Choy

Choy is an assistant manager for a Lens and Shutter retail outlet located in North Vancouver. He studied at New York Institute of Photography in a two-year program. Although he has done free-lance work for advertising and billboard clients, he is most interested in portraiture.

David Cooper

Cooper is a free-lance photographer specializing in the performing arts. Born in Toronto, he studied architecture at the University of Toronto before moving to Vancouver to work as a graphic designer and photographer. Cooper is recognized as one of the leading theatre and dance photographers in the country. He works for the Royal Winnipeg Ballet, Shaw Festival, the Stratford Festival, and many other Vancouver performing groups.

Chris Czartoryski

Czartoryski received a degree in history at Notre Dame University, Nelson, B.C. He later received a diploma from Banff School of Fine Arts in Alberta, where he became an instructor. From there he moved to Vancouver to become a photography teacher at Emily Carr College of Art and Design. Along with teaching, Czartoryski free-lances and has a special interest in the history and criticism of photography.

P. Andras Dancs

A resident of Vancouver for the past five years and a commercial photographer with North Light Images, Dancs has won numerous awards and is included in the permanent collection of the National Archives of Canada. In 1985 the Professional Photographers of Canada granted him the highest award for commercial illustration and feature publicity photography.

Heather Dean

A native Vancouverite, Dean is a self-taught commercial photographer specializing in aerial and location photography. Her work has appeared in national and consumer magazines. Although she travels extensively, Dean says Vancouver will always be one of the most attractive and exciting places to photograph and live.

Stuart Dee

A University of British Columbia graduate, Dee has been working in the commercial photography field for eight years. He is interested in a career as an art photographer.

Darrell Dugàs

Dugàs studied photography at Vancouver College. He is presently employed as a camera technician in the graphic arts field. Dugàs uses 35mm and 4 × 5-inch camera formats and has won several national and international photo contests.

Koos Dykstra

Dykstra has been a free-lance photographer for 11 years. His photographs have been published in Vancouver newspapers as well as *Time, Maclean's, Reader's Digest, Westworld, Western Living,* and *Beautiful B.C.* Dykstra also does brochure and calendar work.

Glen Erickson

Vancouver's lively arts have been photographed by Erickson for more than 10 years. He works primarily for the Arts Club Theatre, New Play Centre, City Stage, Vancouver Symphony Orchestra, and the Vancouver Opera. He also does a great deal of work for individual performers and small theatre groups.

Ed Gifford

Gifford obtained his liberal arts degree from the University of New Mexico, then moved to Canada in 1974. He specializes in corporate communications and advertising. Gifford teaches photography at the University of British Columbia's continuing education program and gives lectures and workshops to students at Emily Carr College of Art and Design. His clients include Benson & Hedges Imperial Tobacco, Nissan of Canada, Tourism B.C., MacMillan Bloedel, Canadian Government Office of Tourism, Honeywell Computer Systems, and C.P. Air.

Larry Goldstein

Goldstein is a self-taught photographer from Montreal. He began his career at a newspaper and now works for many corporate, advertising, and audio-visual clients. Goldstein's photos have been published in local and national magazines.

Jim Harrison

After spending 15 years in hotel management, Harrison became a free-lance photojournalist. His work has appeared in major Canadian daily newspapers as well as Canadian Press and United Press Canada. Harrison's photos can also be seen regularly in the Vancouver *Courier.* He is a member of the National Press Photographers' Association and the International Sporting Press Association.

Al Harvey

Harvey is a veteran of the photography business. His preferred areas are audio-visual and stock photography. Photography is his "vocation and vacation for life." Harvey houses his stock photo collection in his Vancouver home as well as the Masterfile stock photo agency in Toronto. Harvey participated in the book projects *A Day in the Life of Canada* and *A Day in the Life of Japan.*

Kharen Hill

Hill is a New Zealander who has photographed in Europe, Asia, India, the Caribbean, and North America. She works for Air Canada, C.P. Air, Esso, Coca-Cola, IBM, Kodak, the Canadian government, the Vancouver Opera, and the *Financial Times.* She has done stills for Telefilm Canada.

Gerry Kahrmann

A staff photographer with *The Province,* Kahrmann has also worked for the Richmond *Review,* the Coquitlam *Herald,* the Surrey-Delta *Messenger,* the Calgary *Sun,* and as a stringer for United Press Canada. He has been a photojournalist for five years.

Anita Kallberg

Kallberg enjoys careers as an accountant, photographer, wife, and mother. She works closely with her husband, Kent, covering news and sports events in Vancouver and the Lower Mainland.

Kent Kallberg

Combining two professions, Kallberg has worked as a broadcaster as well as photographer for more than 10 years. He is a staff photographer for the B.C. Lions football club and Canada's World Cup soccer team. Kallberg has a commercial studio in downtown Vancouver.

Dave Kiez

Born in 1961, Kiez began his career after a one-year photographic study in Asia. He now resides in Vancouver, where he is building stock of the Pacific Northwest. Kiez also free-lances for several North American geographical and travel magazines.

Greg Kinch

Kinch is primarily a news and sports photographer who works regularly for *Maclean's,* the Vancouver *Sun,* and *Sunday News Magazine.* He has been published in newspapers worldwide through Reuters News Pictures Service.

Andrew Klaver

Klaver likes to photograph people. For him, faces and their subtleties stimulate his ability and awareness. Photography allows him to explore other peoples' lives and thus enrich his own.

Joseph Lederer

As one of the primary still photographers for Vancouver's motion picture industry, "Foto Jo" has done work for films such as "Rocky IV," "First Blood," "Star 80," "Running Brave," "Clan of the Cave Bear," and "The Boy Who Could Fly." Lederer is also known for his corporate and advertising photography.

Ron Long

At Ryerson Polytechnic Institute in Toronto, Long studied photographic arts. He now works in the instructional media centre at Simon Fraser University and teaches photography at night schools and camera clubs throughout Vancouver. Long is an authority on B.C. wild flowers, having photographed and identified 1,000 species to date. He has lectured extensively on botanical subjects.

Stuart McCall

A commercial photographer with North Light Images and a resident of Vancouver for the past six years, McCall's award-winning work has taken him to over 30 countries. Included among McCall's clients are Canadian Pacific Railways, Crown Forest Industries, and Southam Canada.

Neil McDaniel

McDaniel has been scuba diving for 17 years. He combines photography and his background as a marine biologist with his Vancouver-based consultancy and photo agency. McDaniel finds the challenge of underwater photography irresistible. "It's a tough environment to shoot in, but the variety of subjects is endless. It's a shame that so few of us get to see it." McDaniel's work appears regularly in periodicals, textbooks, and other publications on sea life and coastal ecology.

Andrew Metten

Metten has been a photographer for 20 years. A structural engineer with a Vancouver consulting firm, he is also interested in travel and has covered most of the Pacific Rim. Metten's photos have been published in the Vancouver *Sun's* travel section, and his reviews of travel guides appear regularly in *Great Expectations.*

Derik Murray

Murray has operated a studio in Vancouver for more than 10 years. He has won the New York Art Director's Award and two National CAPOC awards. He is also represented in the *1985 Communication Arts Photography Annual.* He maintains an executive position with the Western Magazine awards and serves annually as a judge in the visual categories for the Juno Awards. Murray's work has earned him a national client base.

Albert Normandin

Normandin worked as a technical specialist in the graphic arts industry in Vancouver for 10 years before moving to New York, where he worked and studied under photographer Jay Maisel. After three years, he returned to Vancouver as a free-lance photographer. Normandin has had photos published in *A Day in the Life of Canada, Communication Arts Photography Annual, Popular Photography, SLR Annual,* and *Equity* magazine. He is also recognized for his work in visual arts, annual reports, and advertising.

Patrick Parenteau

In 1982, Parenteau received his first camera as a gift from his wife. Today he is listed with Masterfile Stock Agency in Toronto. He specializes in photojournalism and aerial photography. Parenteau's clients include Canadian Tire, Sun Rype, Datsun, and Expo 86.

Tim Pelling

Pelling is a Vancouver photographer and sculptor. A graduate of Emily Carr College of Art and Design, Pelling works as a free-lance photographer and is involved primarily in editorial and industrial work.

Terry Peters

Born in Toronto in 1954, Peters left home to travel in 1978. After five years he settled in Vancouver, where he began working as a photographer for the *North Shore News.* Today he heads the paper's photo department.

Marin Petkov

Petkov became interested in photography 11 years ago, while traveling. In 1975, he settled in Vancouver, where he began to work on cityscapes and scenic photography. His work now appears on postcards and in books throughout Vancouver. Petkov does free-lance photography.

Martin Roland

The B.C. Pavilion of Expo 86, the *Toronto Star,* Delta Hotels, and Imperial Oil are some of Roland's clients. Both his commercial and personal work have been exhibited in Vancouver.

Colin Savage

An employee of the *Province* newspapers photo department, Savage specializes in remote control applications of cameras. He has designed a remote control system for up to six cameras using infrared, radio control and wire control cameras. He has also designed and patented a high-powered battery pack that he sells to photographers across Canada and the United States.

Stefan Schulhof
Schulhof's clients include B.C. Tel., MacDonald's, B.C. Place Stadium, and Expo 86. He is also a member of the Professional Photographers of Canada.

Steve Short
In 1982, Short began selling his photographs of horses to help pay for film costs. At one point a horse was given to him in payment for pictures. Today he owns several horses and his photographic career helps pay for their stable and feed bills.

Anji Smith
Smith is studying photojournalism at Emily Carr College of Art and Design in Vancouver. She is also an apprentice lab technician and custom black-and-white printer for Spotty Dog Photographic Labs. She is gaining technical experience at the Dolores Baswick Photographic studio in Gastown, Vancouver.

Michele Smith
Once a make-up artist for television, Smith became interested in fashion photography while working as an assistant to others in the field. Smith's ambition led her to Paris, where she worked for a large commercial studio. She has now established herself as a highly successful fashion photographer in Vancouver.

Brian Stablyk
A graduate of the University of British Columbia in the fine arts studio program, Stablyk worked exclusively in photography. One year of graduate-level study in communications followed, as well as numerous photographic exhibitions. Stablyk has become a widely published free-lance photographer and has a stock library of the Pacific Northwest numbering more than 100,000 images.

Naomi Stevens
Since graduating from Brooks Institute of photography, Stevens has worked in film and audio-visual productions. She currently free-lances in Vancouver, specializing in aerial photography for corporate, audio-visual, and editorial clients.

Tom Sutherland
Sutherland conceived, produced, and directed *Vancouver: A Year in Motion.* As a working photojournalist for 15 years, his work has been published in international magazines including *Vogue, Ski, Powder,* and *Surfing.* His experience in a variety of publishing and advertising ventures as the owner of *The Whistler Question* newspaper and publisher of the magazine *Winter Tracks* increased the expertise he brought to this project. Sutherland lives and works in Vancouver.

Lloyd Sutton
Working as a free-lance photographer for the past four years, Sutton has established a client base throughout Western Canada. He travels extensively on tourism and industrial assignments.

Stephe Tate
Originally from Mercer Island, Washington, Tate moved to Vancouver in 1970, where he attended Vancouver Community College-Langara Campus and studied formal photography. Tate's work is mainly of the commercial sort and he has won several awards in this area.

Dietmar Waber
After studying at the University of British Columbia and the Vancouver School of Art, Waber taught graphics for seven years at Vancouver Senior Secondary School. In 1983 he turned to landscape photography as a full-time pursuit. Waber now owns and operates the Photo West Gallery in Vancouver's Gastown, where he exhibits land-, sea-, and cityscapes of British Columbia.

Stirling Ward
Ward is a commercial illustrative photographer whose studio is situated in downtown Vancouver. Ward is a renowned photographer with numerous regional, national, and international awards, including being a New York CLIO finalist. As the official marketing photographer for Expo 86, he has captured the essence of the World's Fair on film.

Jane Weitzel
A free-lance photographer since 1980, Weitzel opened her own downtown photography studio in 1981. Currently she is widely published in fashion, advertising, and personality photography. Also an accomplished sports photographer, she specializes in covering windsurfing and special events, including organizing the Vancouver Sea Fest photographers on location.

Perry Zavitz
After three years of studying photography in the East followed by journey to Paris and the American Midwest, Zavitz came to Vancouver to work in the commercial field. He plans to continue free-lancing, and would like to embark on an extensive photographic journey through Asia.

Writers' Biographies

Vicki Gabereau
Gabereau is host of CBC Radio's nightly Vancouver-based interview program, *Gabereau,* formerly *Variety Tonight.* She has been called "the most amusing woman working in radio in Canada".

Audrey Grescoe
Grescoe is associate editor of *Western Living.* Her by-line has appeared in *Homemakers, City Woman, The Canadian, Reader's Digest, Financial Post, Your Money,* and *Vancouver* magazines.

Paul Grescoe
Currently a partner in Wheeler Grescoe Communications, Grescoe has served as editor at *Maclean's, Calgary, Edmonton,* and *Vancouver* magazines. He is co-author of *The Money Rustlers: Self-Made Millionaires of the New West.*

Rick Hoogendoorn
Hoogendoorn, a graduate of British Columbia Institute of Technology in broadcast journalism, is a free-lance writer as well as associate producer and reporter at CKVU-TV First News in Vancouver.

James Lawton
Sports columnist for the Vancouver *Sun,* Lawton is author of the best-seller *Tiger: A Hockey Story* and is currently preparing a book on high-jumper Debbie Brill.

Scott Mowbray
Mowbray is a CBC restaurant critic and co-author of *The 1986 Guide to Vancouver.* His work has appeared in *Western Living, Vancouver, Cuisine, The Globe and Mail, The Sun* and *The Province.*

Anne Petrie
Author of *Ethnic Vancouver, Vancouver Secrets,* and *More Vancouver Secrets,* Petrie is also a free-lance broadcaster who appears regularly on CBC-TV's "Midday" and CBC Radio's "Morningside."

Barbara Pettit
Pettit has been writing a column on architecture for the Vancouver *Sun* for the past two years. Originally a journalist, she also has a background in architecture and environmental studies.

Timothy Renshaw
Renshaw works as a reporter and restaurant critic for the *North Shore News.* A free-lance writer since 1982, he has sold articles and editorials to a variety of local and national newspapers and magazines. In 1983, he wrote and co-produced his first book, *Polar Bear,* an historical chronicle of Vancouver's Polar Bear Swim.

Duncan Stacey
Stacey is an industrial historian specializing in the fishing industry. An experienced commercial fisherman, he writes frequently on the history and current issues of British Columbia fisheries.

Carole Taylor
Taylor is heard regularly on "Inside Expo," a program featured on 350 radio stations across North America. She is a veteran of 20 years in broadcasting, including "W5" and "Canada AM."

Don Whiteley
The forestry writer for the Vancouver *Sun,* Whiteley has also worked for the Ottawa *Journal,* the Calgary *Herald,* the Calgary *Albertan,* radio station CFAC in Calgary and the Boston *Globe.*

Rosemary Wurts
A free-lance writer for three years, Wurts has published work in the *Financial Post Magazine, Writer's Digest, The Globe and Mail,* and *Your Money.* Her articles cover a wide range of topics, including travel, personal finance, lifestyles, and the arts.

Paul Yee
Yee is an archivist with the Vancouver City Archives. A specialist in Chinese-Canadian history, he has written numerous articles, children's books, and radio features.

Vancouver: A Year in Motion Staff

Produced and Directed by
Tom Sutherland
Cindy Bellamy

Project Manager and Art Director
Leslie Smolan
Carbone Smolan Associates

**Associate Project Manager
and Art Director**
Thomas K. Walker
Carbone Smolan Associates

Associate Designer
Emily Singer

Editor
Denise Bukowski

Copy Editors
Kathy Berger
Newsweek
Florence Kurzman

Editorial Research
Rick Hoogendoorn
Terry Konkin
Scott Mowbray
Barbara Pettit
Terry Renshaw
Timothy Renshaw
Rosemary Wurts

Editorial Consultants
Rita D. Jacobs, Ph.D.
Emily Singer

Picture Editors
Leslie Smolan
Carbone Smolan Associates
Thomas K. Walker
Carbone Smolan Associates

Office Manager
Grace Bellamy

**Production Director,
Foreword Page**
Rob Scott

Legal Advisors
Stephen Cheng
Legal
Leonard Polsky
Trademark

Collins Publishers, Canada
Nicholas Harris
President
Janice Whitford
Editorial Director
Bill Connor
Sales Director

Western Sales Representatives
David Harding
Phillip Rutherford
Keith Sacre

Publication Consultants
David Cohen
Rick Smolan

Dai Nippon Printing
Takeshi Fukunaga
Vice President/New York
Kimio Honda
Project Manager/New York
Fumiya Chiba
Project Manager/Tokyo

Horizon Type, Inc.
Bob Burns
President
Noreen Bartolomeo
Curt Belshe
George Bohn
John Caventer
Robert Davidson
Adrienne Belle Eisenberg
Joanne Horenstein
Leah Jacobs
Michelle Lockhart
Fran Luck
Daisann McLane
Ruth Ruston
Lori Schulman

**Vancouver: A Year In Motion
Documentary Production**

Executive Producers
Tom Sutherland
Cindy Bellamy

Producer
Craig Sawchuk
Vidatron Communications

Editor
Jane Morrison

Cinematographers
Robert Ennis
Bob Asgeirsson
Hugh Beard
Curtis Petersen
Tim Sale

Camera Assistants
Doug Pruss
Joel Ransom

Sound
Gordon Anderson
Michael McGee
Karen Kostenko

Vancouver:
A Year in Motion
Friends, Advisors and
Consultants

Abbotsford Air Show
ABC Photocolour
Helen Adams
Peter Alpen
Andre's Wine
Ariel Sports
Randy Baker
Beth Bangor
Doug Banner
Elizabeth Bayer
BCTV
Hugh Beard
Ruby Beckett
Brian Belgasic
Grace Bellamy
Peter Bellamy
Chubb Berry
Tom Best
Harvey Blackmore
Jim Blair
Harry Bosley
Randy Bradley
Anthony Brpic
Burrard Air
B.C. Ferries
B.C. Rail
Camp Capilano
Canadian Broadcasting Corporation
Canadian Coast Guard—Hovercraft Base
Capilano Fish Hatchery
Diane Marie Carbone
Raymond Chow
Don Clerke
Gerry Collins
Violet Collins
Loraleigh Conlinn
Brian Cruickshank
Chris Dahl
Danger Bay Productions
Stuart Davis
Chuck Davis
John Dickinson
Kevin Doyle
Bob Dubberley
Murray Duncan
Harvey Dupré
Giselle Dupuis
Deni Eagland
Alistair Eagle
Dick Elke
Evergreen Sportswear
Jeff Fargher
Fiddlesticks Hair Fashions
Peter Folkes
Foto Fun Cameras
Tony Gallagher
Harry & Pauline Gerbracht
David Graham
David Gray
Lorne Greenberg
George Greenwood
Greg Griffiths
Grouse Mountain Resorts
Jack Guest
Patrick Hattenberger
Hawthorne Lodge
Monica Hayes
Craig Hodge
Eileen Hoeter
Saralee James
Henry Janz
Nomi Kaplan
Josh Keller
Dennis Knutsen
Kopernik Lodge
Frank Laleune
Le Crocodile Restaurant
Eddie Lee
Jeannie Lee
Lens and Shutter
Ken Lieberman Laboratories, Inc.
Hari Lila

Peter Little
Karen Love
John Lund
Joe Martin
Pamela Martin
Glenn McCullough
Bill McInnes
Target Media
Ann Marie Metten
Molson Brewery
Michael Morissette
Ann Mortifee
Allison Muench
Jack Murray
Henry Myers
Alice Niwinski
North Shore News
Ocean Fisheries
Bev Olandt
Toni Onley
Pacific Coliseum
Pappas Furs
Rose Peijnenburg
Dick Phillips
Ingrid Plaudis
Presentation House
The Province
Purdy's Chocolates
Queen Mary Community School
Afarin Radjaei
RCMP Airport Detachment
Harry Reid
Bill Reid
Terry Renshaw
Gord Robertson
Rocky IV Productions
Carolyn Rutledge and Family
Craig Sawchuk
Simon Scott
Anthony Semma
Eleni Skalbania
Neil Snape
Social Planning Dept. City Hall
Sue Stewart
Students and Staff of Jericho Hill School
Carolyn Sullivan
Doris-Kay Sutherland
Douglas Sutherland
Richard Swiecki
Claire Taylor
Vancouver Chapter of the Guardian Angels
Vancouver City Police, Mounted Squad
Vancouver General Hospital
Vancouver Helicopters
Vancouver International Airport
  Area Control Centre
Vancouver International Airport
  Fire Department
Vancouver Magazine
Vancóuver Public Aquarium
Vancouver Public Library
Vancouver Science Centre
The Vancouver Sun
Versatile Pacific Shipyards
Dale Walters
Len Walters
Ray Walters
Jerry Watson
Nancy Weatherley
Marion Webber
West Bay Elementary School
West Vancouver Municipality
Blake Williams
Wyland
Paul Yee
Dana Zalko